DESIGNING
ROOMS FOR CHILDREN

DESIGNING
ROOMS FOR CHILDREN

MARY GILLIATT

LITTLE, BROWN AND COMPANY

BOSTON   TORONTO   LONDON

Original room designs created by Mary Gilliatt
and illustrated by Ross Wardle/Tudor Art Studios
and Ken Hollins

Special photography by Michael Dunne

LIBRARY OF CONGRESS CATALOG CARD
NO. 84-52849

FIRST PAPERBACK EDITION 1990
10 9 8 7 6 5 4 3 2 1

Published simultaneously in Canada
by Little, Brown & Company (Canada) Limited

Printed in Italy

Planning a child's room may sound an easy and delightful thing to do. First-time parents can dwell romantically on such thoughts as cribs hung with sprigged muslin, nursery teas by a glowing fire, shafts of morning sunlight and a general happy-ever-after feeling. There's no harm in dreaming, but these ideas have to be juggled with practicalities, such as space available, cash in the bank and the fact that the babe in the cot is going to grow up, sooner rather than later. Between the baby in the crib and the teenager with the computer game there are going to be several major changes and stages, each of which is going to make very different demands on that room, and all of which will be upon you before you can make major plans to redecorate every time.

Children's rooms present more of a forward planning exercise than just about any other room in the house except for the kitchen. And so they should. After all, if you are hoping to make the space look good, and serve a useful purpose over the maximum number of years for the minimum expenditure, you're asking a lot and you won't achieve it without first giving very careful consideration to the problems involved.

Right at the beginning you must think far ahead and plan for modifications to be made over the years: how cribs must give way to cots, cots to beds, toy cupboards to wardrobes, play surfaces to desks. You can't anticipate every detail of games or electronic equipment that may be wanted in ten year's time, but you can ensure a degree of flexibility in the space they will occupy.

So, before you go overboard for that miniature paradise, stop and think. There are lots of ways to accommodate the necessary alter-ations over the years, to keep up with your children's progress and avoid having to discard too much of your original investment. That's what this book is all about.

The choice of decorative schemes for a child's room can be another stumbling block to parents who are concerned about the possible effect – good or bad – on their offspring. So much is written about the importance of environment to a growing child, the necessity for a stimulating background or a restful one, that some parents are afraid of making a terrible mistake over colours and furnishings. How can you make a room that is fun by day and calming by night? How can you create the sort of room that will help children to develop their creative abilities, give them all the stimulation they need, and still leave room for them to add their own stamp when they are ready for it? How can you be certain that everything you have chosen is safe? That there are no hidden pitfalls and traps? Above all, how can you avoid making mistakes when there is little money or time to set them right?

The purpose of this book is to reassure and inspire: not to promise miracles but to show good ideas at work and explain how they were achieved. There is no blueprint for the ideal children's room but there is plenty of good, practical advice that you can profit by and any amount of options to choose from. All of them are aimed at giving you some measure of confidence, for that is the most important element that you can bring to any sort of decoration. With confidence, you can plan a sensible, adaptable framework that can be dressed up or played down — a room that will successfully serve both you and your children for many years to come.

This stylish high-tech bedroom-workroom looks spacious as well as saving space. Note the way colour defines territories and desks are slipped under bunks.

The old-fashioned nursery had the right basic ideas. It was essentially a room given over to children for which most parents were content to provide, if they could, a well-ventilated space with somewhere to sleep, plenty of floor/play space, somewhere to sit, some sort of games, drawing, work surface and reasonable storage.

In a sense this sort of framework is still in force today — but with some big differences. First, many of the clever and colourful ideas produced for nursery and primary schools to provide intellectual stimulus for their pupils have begun to trickle back into the home in the form of educational playthings, body-building structures and early learning apparatus. And second, children today belong to a technologically sophisticated generation where the computer is becoming as commonplace as the television, and where audio-visual equipment replaces building bricks and snakes and ladders almost as a matter of course.

This means that any forward planning at the infant stage should involve thinking at least about the probability of having to make room for such things. While it is impos-

sible to project several years ahead and visualize exactly what amazing new inventions are going to invade our lives, let alone what size and shape they are going to be or how many extra electric points and outlets they'll need, what you *can* do is think in terms of flexible arrangements in the home.

Parents of young infants will find it difficult to imagine anything at all beyond the immediate world of nappies and feeds, cots and baths but it doesn't last for ever and if that's all they've planned for, they'll find the room soon outgrown and unsuitable for the next stage in their children's lives. The time, money and effort spent on creating a room the children don't want to use will be wasted.

So, when you are faced with this empty room that you want to take care of your children's needs for the next eighteen years, remember, as you make your plans, that adaptability is the name of the game.

Simple red-painted units, left, define space and set the style in a teenager's room. Multi-coloured vertical blinds are matched by cushions. Trompe l'oeil window is fun in a small kid's space, right.

From nursery to bedsit

Stage 1 – Infancy *Simple hard-wearing drawers and wardrobe make a basic framework on which to build, and provide valuable storage space. Rubber stud flooring is non-slip, easy to clean and keeps noise down. The trolley keeps baby accessories neat and tidy. Wall lights on a dimmer switch and a light-resistant roller-blind help to ensure peaceful nights.*

Stage 2 – Toddlers and pre-school *Safety becomes vital as toddlers grow up. Prevent accidents by fitting a bed rail, window bars and socket covers. Encourage artists with a blackboard fixed below the dado rail, and promote tidiness by providing a large chest for toys.*

Stage 3 – Early school days *Freshen up the room with a new rug, poster, blind and curtains. Modular bunk beds accommodate friends, and the work surface and trolley now house more grown-up accessories.*

Stage 4 – Secondary school *Older children value privacy and a bedroom doubles as a study/sitting room with the aid of convertible sofa-beds. Good lighting is provided for serious homework and the shelves are now devoted to books. The dado rail is removed and a fitted carpet suits sophisticated teenage tastes.*

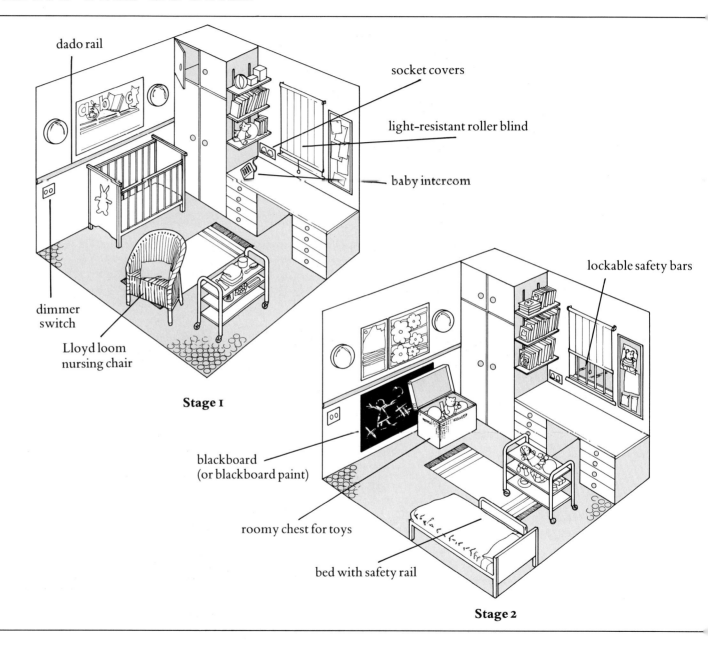

dado rail

socket covers

light-resistant roller blind

baby intercom

dimmer switch

Lloyd loom nursing chair

Stage 1

lockable safety bars

blackboard (or blackboard paint)

roomy chest for toys

bed with safety rail

Stage 2

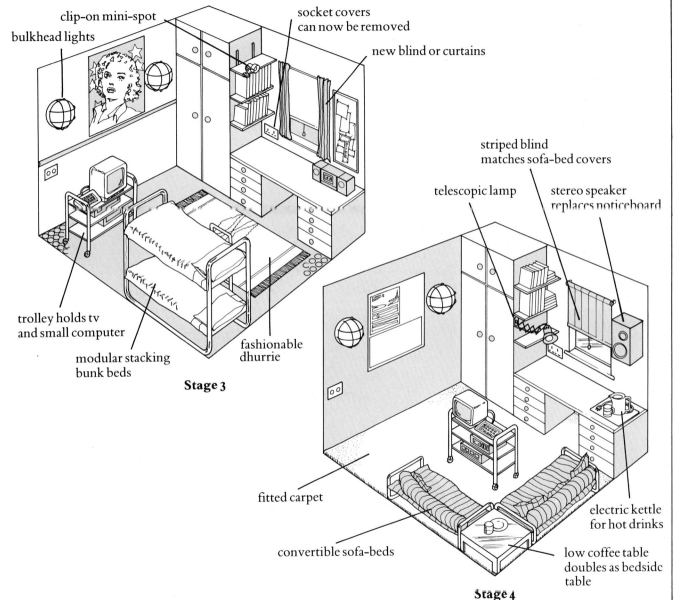

clip-on mini-spot

bulkhead lights

socket covers
can now be removed

new blind or curtains

trolley holds tv
and small computer

modular stacking
bunk beds

fashionable
dhurrie

Stage 3

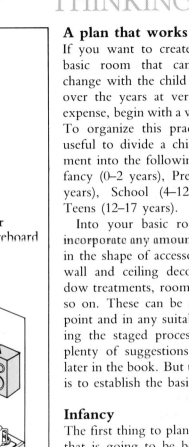

striped blind
matches sofa-bed covers

telescopic lamp

stereo speaker
replaces noticeboard

fitted carpet

convertible sofa-beds

electric kettle
for hot drinks

low coffee table
doubles as bedside
table

Stage 4

A plan that works

If you want to create the sort of basic room that can grow and change with the child (or children) over the years at very little extra expense, begin with a working plan. To organize this practically, it is useful to divide a child's development into the following stages: Infancy (0–2 years), Pre-School (2–4 years), School (4–12 years) and Teens (12–17 years).

Into your basic room you can incorporate any amount of fun ideas in the shape of accessories, fabrics, wall and ceiling decoration, window treatments, room dividers and so on. These can be added at any point and in any suitable style during the staged process. There are plenty of suggestions about them later in the book. But the first thing is to establish the basics.

Infancy

The first thing to plan in any room that is going to be both bedroom and play space is storage. Children, even babies, have a lot of belongings — toys, clothes and equipment of various kinds — that are going to accumulate with the years. Where are you going to put it all?

For an average, say 4 × 3 metre (12 × 10 ft) room that has no existing cupboards, either build in a full-length double cupboard, floor to ceiling, or buy a sturdy, roomy second-hand wardrobe. It really is

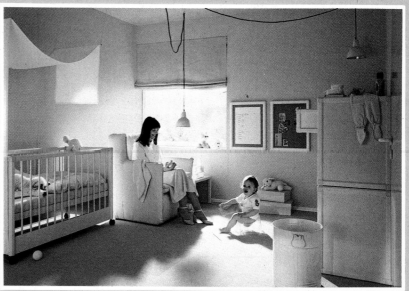

Clear colours, adequate storage, good lighting, sturdy flooring, these are the major considerations in any child's room. Above left: Interesting transparent-sided cot takes centre stage and picks up room colours. Above: Light cords are looped from a central ceiling point to place light where it's wanted most. Far left: Flexible storage and warm colours will look right in this room for many years. Cot can give way to bed later, but striped blind and cushions can stay. Left: The abacus under the work surface is perfectly placed for a small child as well as looking decorative.

false economy to bother with any of those specially built mini cupboards that may look rather sweet but become obsolete in no time at all.

In the very early stages, your basic cupboard/wardrobe can be divided in two. Use one side for hanging space, with perhaps one rail at waist level and either another rail or removable shelves above. These can be removed as the child's clothes get larger and longer. Fit the other side with well-spaced shelves and use it for toy storage; later on it will be useful for sweaters, shirts and a lot of chunky, bulky clothing.

You will also need at least two chests of drawers. Unpainted wooden chests of drawers are inexpensive and perfectly adequate. Set them against the wall leaving a knee-hole space in between (to form an eventual desk/dressing table) and top them with some sort of easily cleanable laminate surface. If these can run along the length of one whole wall so much the better: such an arrangement looks neat and tidy and these are words you are going to be using a lot over the next ten years.

The drawers can be used for nappies, night clothes, underwear, talc and all the other baby necessities in the beginning as well as for an overflow of toys. Later the same drawers will take other clothes, other toys, other games, school work and general clutter.

The same work surfaces that serve so well for changing nappies on, can later be used for playing on and, when the child is older still, they make ideal desks and dressing tables. Here, light grey and white wallpaper and curtains, combined with white furniture and bed linen, help to enlarge visually a relatively small space.

The long run of work surface along the top of the chests can first be used for changing the baby, then for play (painting, drawing, cutting out) and later still for school work and displaying possessions. The actual chests can be painted, lacquered or otherwise decorated, many times over the years in whatever style happens to be in keeping at the time.

Against the wall behind and above these units it would be a good idea to build a series of shelves or shelves and lockers interspersed with pinboards and space for drawing and the inevitable posters and pictures of pop stars. Make sure all drawing pins are out of reach of toddlers.

In the first instance, shelves can hold soft toys later giving way to books, records, files. The pinboard takes progress charts and nursery information to start with and can carry on into school years to provide space for homework timetables and general reminders.

Well planned lighting

The lighting should also be planned at this stage. Begin with simple wall lights on a dimmer switch. These have two advantages: they can be turned right down at night and the fact that they are built into the wall means that there are no wires or cords for a child to tamper with or trip over. Moreover, this sort of light will be far pleasanter than that given by a central ceiling pendant.

At the same time, at least six other outlets should be provided: two of them above the work surface and the others in corners but placed above a crawling child's reach and safely fitted with shutters.

Simple Venetian blinds at the window will filter the light during the day at rest times — or use roller blinds backed with suitable black-out material.

Flooring

This completes the background except for the floor covering which is discussed in detail on pages 41-45. At this stage it is enough to stress that the most sensible floors should be hardwearing and easy to clean but not uncomfortable or cold or noisy. Young children spend a lot of time on the floor, sitting, crawling, lying, playing, so the covering is important. Fortunately there are plenty to choose from: planed-down and polyurethaned wood, vinyl-coated cork tiles, cushioned vinyl tiles, linoleum.

If you are going to put rugs on hard floor surfaces, make sure they are held in place with a non-slip backing; on fitted carpet they can be prevented from rucking with strips of Velcro touch-and-close fastening stitched to the back – use only the hooked side of the strip so that it will catch on the carpet tufts or loops.

Free-standing furnishings

When the baby is very small you may want to use a crib or cradle for him or her to sleep in. These should be abandoned in favour of a cot (which has greater stability) as soon as the child can sit independently – usually at about 5-7 months. A cot should be sturdily built and thoroughly safe, which means making sure that slats are not more than 6 cm (2 ⅜in) apart, that the top rails are an adequate height for protection (i.e. preventing the child falling out even when the side is lowered), that the drop-sides themselves are

The need to plan for the future has produced this inventive idea for adaptable work surfaces. As the child grows, so the desk top can be raised to an appropriate height. The blue paint gives a sense of unity to the odd assembly of furniture.

the sort that cannot be released by a child and that the mattress is firm and a perfect fit so that there are no dangerous gaps between it and the cot sides. Look for BS 1753 when buying a new cot and see page 83 for more details.

Apart from the crib or cot you'll need very little furniture. At the infant stage a trolley is a godsend (especially if it has a wheel lock) because it is versatile and moveable. You can wheel it about to have it at your elbow wherever you need it; with a baby on your lap you can't be leaping up and down for things you've forgotten — the furniture has to come to you. Move the trolley by the crib or cot, use it as a stand for a baby bath or scales or general washing kit. Move it into the bathroom at bath time, if that is where you bath the baby. Later it can hold games, a tv, hi-fi, even a computer.

Another useful item at this stage is a cane or old wooden rocker or other nice capacious chair which will last through all the stages and possibly only need re-cushioning occasionally as opposed to re-covering. Do choose one which does not constrict your elbows, to make feeding easier.

Pre-school 2–4

Now the room has to cope with a bigger child who is up and around and into everything.

The window can be left much as it is (with Venetian blinds or black-out backed roller blinds) so that the day does not start too early for parents, daytime resting is made easier and any sun can easily be filtered. However, it is a good idea to fit some vertical bars not more than 6 cm (2⅜ in) apart (which can be removed later) to prevent any unsupervised adventuring and possible accidents. It is essential that these can be easily removed in case of fire. Bars with keys are available.

Because children at this age can't concentrate for long on any one thing they need lots of playthings and you are liable to have a great overflow of toys. Make a home for these in an old wooden chest which could later act as a coffee table, or with tough polyurethane or corrugated cardboard storage boxes which can double as play equipment and become trains, carriages, trolleys or anything the child likes to make them in his imagination. Stacking boxes and trays are also good ideas. And, unless there's another baby, the trolley, denuded of all the infant paraphernalia, can also help to cope with all the toys and games. A portable Moses basket or basket carry cot are both useful for storing soft toys. They can also be used for transporting toys into another room, if necessary.

About halfway through this stage the cot can be replaced by a pair of

Above: A trolley is almost indispensable in a baby's room, not only for storing all the necessary paraphernalia, but also for its ability to be moved where it's wanted. Later it can be used to hold a tv, hi-fi or general washing kit for children lucky enough to have their own washbasins.

Right: Totally secure bunk beds for very young children will enable you to sleep better at night too. There is no chance of little bodies rolling on to the floor from great heights here. The fresh pink and blue paint helps to relieve the rather cage-like atmosphere. The same colours are also used for the lights and bed linen.

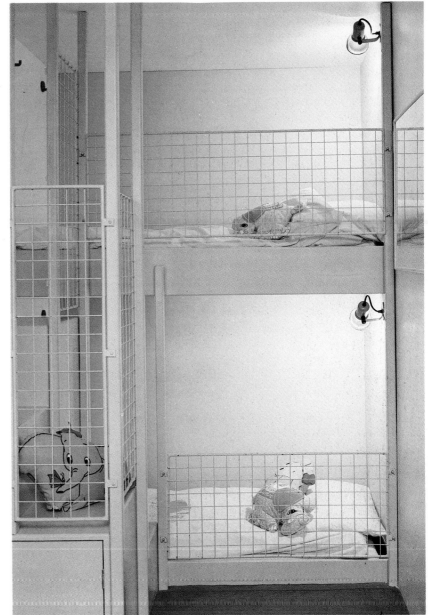

15

modular bunk beds of the kind that can be dismantled and turned into ordinary single beds. The second bunk will come into play either for a second child or for a friend and provide a two-tiered play area as well. Some bunk beds have a useful drawer underneath for even more storage; buy this kind if you are pressed for space.

Even homework can be fun in the right setting. Drawers, a cupboard, and kneehole spaces topped by a long shelf make a practical desk for two.

School 4–12

Now the second rod can be removed from the wardrobe to leave full-length hanging space. You can dispense with window bars. The play top is going to do double duty as part-time work top so, to ease the transition, add an angled light for homework. A couple of upright chairs can come in at this stage. The pinboard can stay, and the trolley will now become useful for holding models, games, perhaps a tv set or a small home computer to amuse a child and to help with learning.

Teens 12–17

The bunk beds can now be dismantled and turned into two single beds. If space permits, place the beds at right angles to one another and put a small low table between them, to serve both. By day turn the beds into sofas by adding tailored covers, some bolsters and cushions.

The floor may need some attention too; it could be carpeted or covered with matting or painted and stencilled. Or you could simply add one or two rugs.

Window blinds can be changed

for a new fabric roller or curtains and walls re-painted, papered or otherwise decorated to the teenager's wishes.

Teenagers have very much more sophisticated needs than younger children. They will more than likely feel the need to make their room into a bed-sitting room of some kind. Extra seating, in the form of bean bags or covered foam slabs, is reasonably cheap and always seems popular since it is less formal. Or a spare comfortable armchair, if you have the space, makes a comfortable

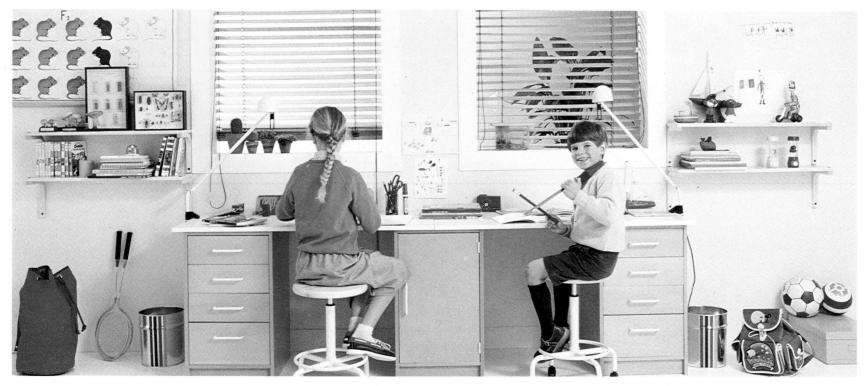

place to sit and read. Cover the bed with a fitted cover and scatter cushions to turn it into a sofa by day. If space is short, provide a large kneehole dressing-table which can double as a desk. Otherwise, television sets, cassette players, computers and school books can be placed on the laminated work surface. A more extensive wardrobe, musical and electronic equipment (guitars, synthesisers and so on) will maximise the need for good storage.

With any teenager, it is a good idea to install a washbasin in the room, to discourage them from monopolizing the bathroom! Dressing-room style light fittings around a mirror will be particularly appreciated by girls for make-up practice.

The great thing is that, although the room looks quite different and fulfils changing needs at each stage, the furnishings remain substantially the same over a good number of years. No change of stage costs very much money, except perhaps for the final transformation.

As well as being very budget-conscious, such a plan is highly flexible. It allows first the parents and then the child himself enormous scope for adding, changing and indulging individual tastes and interests. As long as the original basic plan is simple and includes plenty of storage a room can go on developing along with the child it caters for.

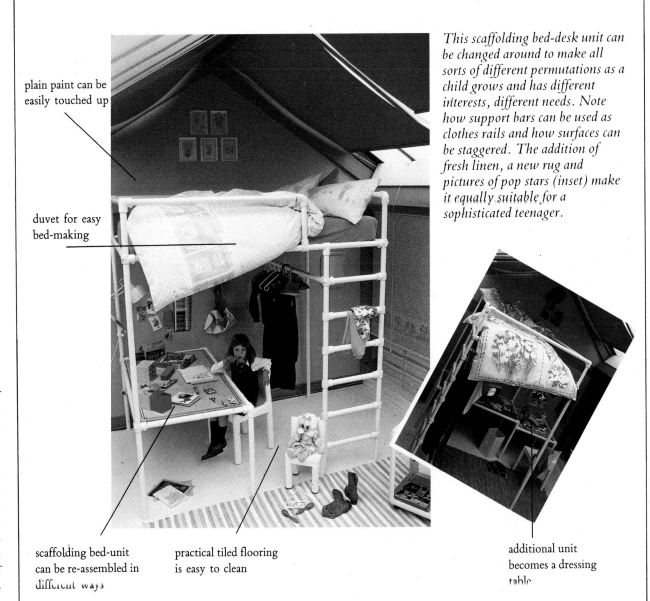

plain paint can be easily touched up

duvet for easy bed-making

This scaffolding bed-desk unit can be changed around to make all sorts of different permutations as a child grows and has different interests, different needs. Note how support bars can be used as clothes rails and how surfaces can be staggered. The addition of fresh linen, a new rug and pictures of pop stars (inset) make it equally suitable for a sophisticated teenager.

scaffolding bed-unit can be re-assembled in different ways

practical tiled flooring is easy to clean

additional unit becomes a dressing table

Before you actually start any decorating at all you must plan out the lighting and heating of your child's room. Any re-wiring and re-routing of electric wiring, should be done well before you put paint to wall, both for aesthetic and practical reasons. Aim to get rid of any trailing wires; apart from looking unsightly they are a safety hazard.

It is equally dangerous to overload too few outlets with too many appliances so make provision now for a generous number of points, ideally no less than six. You will need these in the early stages for bottle warmers, extra heaters and so on, and later for toys and games – trains, racing cars – and any equipment you might want to install such as tv, radio, stereo, video, computer, tape recorder, model-making equipment. Remember this is the age of electronics and it will become more so, not less. Sophisticated gadgets that might seem expensively out of reach now might well be commonplace and much, much cheaper in a very few years.

It might also be a good idea to wire in a baby alarm system with extensions say, in the master bedroom, the kitchen and outside the living room.

If the room already has central heating make sure it is adequate and comfortable. If you are starting from scratch, you will have the opportunity to work out a suitable heating system right from the beginning.

Children's rooms need a lot of light but the type and the amount will vary considerably at each stage of their growth. For example, you should have good overall light for nursing and bathing the baby and for him or her to play by later. In addition you will need lights that can be dimmed right down at night, as a comfort to small children in the dark and so that infants can have their night feeds in a gentle glow which will not disturb them or any older sleeping children; enough light by the cot to enable parents to read bedtime stories; a reading lamp by the bed later on for older chil-

Two ultra-modern rooms make the most of the latest technology and lighting effects: slick yellow and grey room (left) has wisely provided plenty of outlets for stereo, video and computer equipment; climbing frame sleep/play complex (right) is softly and safely lit after dark.

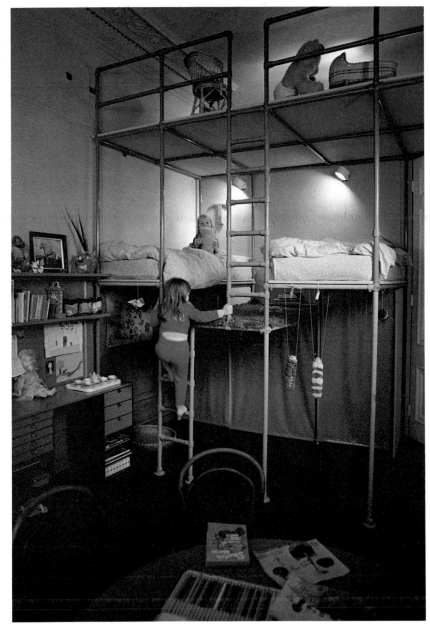

LIGHTING AND HEATING

dren, and good light on the work surface for playing and drawing and later on for homework and study. Individual clip-on lights are a particular good idea for children in bunk beds as they can read at night without disturbing the other child.

General light
Most electricians will automatically install a centre point in the ceiling but try to avoid this if you can unless you are going to use it for track lighting. The sun does not stay still in the middle of the sky all day, so why, if artificial light is meant to emulate daylight, should we always have this often harsh central light?

Evenly spaced wall lights are a much better solution; or recessed ceiling lights set all around the perimeter of the room. Track lighting may not fit your romantic idea of nursery lighting but architects often specify it if used with a dimmer switch. The different components can be fixed to shine in whichever directions they are most needed.

Ideally, different types of lighting should be chosen to suit the many functions of the room. Low-hanging, wide-brimmed shades over the desk area (left) are ideal for study and play, with individual spotlights clipped to handy cubby-hole storage on the wall for bed-time reading. Foldaway Murphy beds provide extra play space during the day.

radiator has been shielded with a cloud-shaped screen to protect child from possible harm

attractive canopy effect over the bed keeps off draughts and encourages a feeling of security

built-in safety rail on a higher-than-average bed is essential for young children

continuous roll of drawing paper and large blackboard save scribbles on the wall

bedside fabric pockets save the bed becoming uncomfortably cluttered with favourite toys

A central pendant light can be better positioned by using a long flex and ceiling hook. This bright, appealing room with handy storage bed (right) now has light where it's needed – over the bed. A row of spotlights highlights the painting and play counter, specially positioned at child height.

sturdy pine beds incorporate useful drawers for storage below

Cheerful practicality

A child's first room needs to be bright and stimulating as well as practical. Careful planning means it can be easily and inexpensively adapted as the child grows, like this room where a row of simple cupboard units provides not only ample worktop surface for changing nappies, but will later be useful for play, study and storing clothes and toys. The room has a red, yellow and green colour scheme: naive flower design on white for the walls, a larger splash of flowers on the window blinds and a red and white grid design vinyl on the floor – all easy-to-clean and practical. Safety is a vital element of design here: electricity sockets are positioned high on the wall, out of reach of toddlers, and provided with covers; windows are protected with lockable bars painted bright green and yellow to match the general colour scheme, while a built-in baby alarm is essential for peace of mind. Lighting has been carefully thought out too with strip lighting at ceiling level behind a bright yellow fascia board and indirect uplighters on the wall, both controlled by dimmer switches for easier night-time feeding. The wall has been painted white between the skirting board and dado rail, to protect the wallpaper from grubby fingers, and there is plenty of room for essentials such as a sturdy cot, covered basket, baby change unit and a nursing chair.

LIGHTING AND HEATING

If you can afford it, a separate circuit of low wattage lights is ideal for a child's room but it is expensive. Whatever you do, try to install dimmer switches so that lights can be dimmed at will and separately, leaving just one light on all night if necessary. Not only is this comforting for the child but it will save running costs.

Task lights

This includes light for the play/work surface and light for reading. Get outlets installed in the appropriate positions so that you can introduce reading and work lamps later. It's advisable to avoid any sort of free-standing lamps; toddlers can easily pull them over. Again, wall lights by the cot or bed would be preferable. If you had cupboards or shelves set over the play/work surface, you could install strip lighting behind a baffle or valance just below

Adjustable lamps and spotlights are especially useful: a large angle-lamp (top left) is ideal for play, with a shielded wall-light for reading in bed. An adjustable fixture doubles for bedside and homework light for an older child (top right). Striped room (right) needs only eyeball ceiling fittings and bedside light (not seen). The small room (far right) uses shiny surfaces to reflect light from one narrow window and a row of adjustable spotlights.

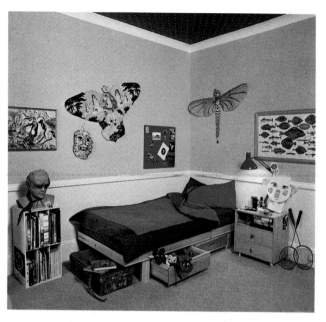

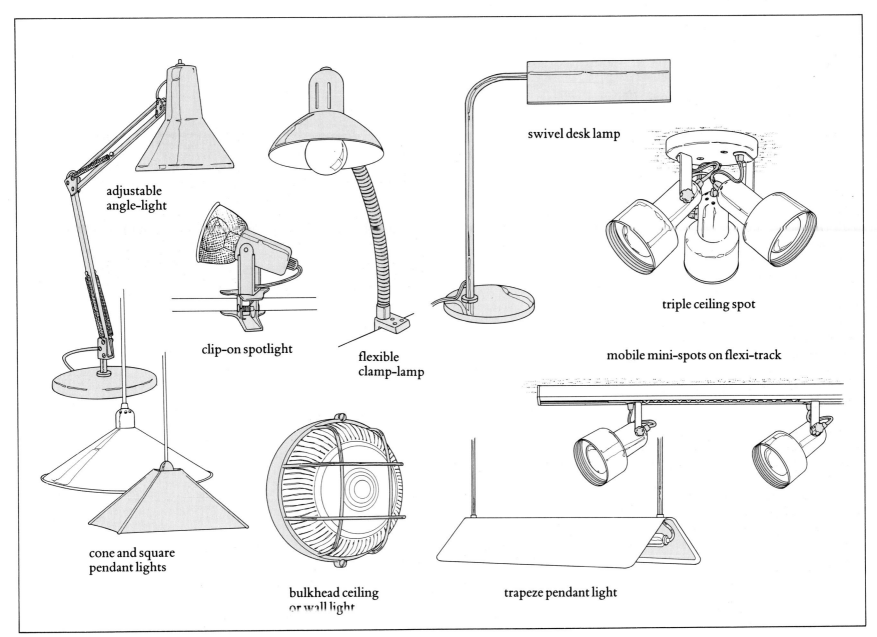

adjustable
angle-light

clip-on spotlight

flexible
clamp-lamp

swivel desk lamp

triple ceiling spot

mobile mini-spots on flexi-track

cone and square
pendant lights

bulkhead ceiling
or wall light

trapeze pendant light

Suspended lights with conical shades on extra-long flexes provide good light over a child's desk (left). Note the large blackboard on the wall for acceptable scribbles and plenty of open storage shelves to match the desk for easily accessible toys and books. The teenage bedroom (above) has a more sophisticated system of small adjustable spotlights and a matching conical shade on a very long flex to hang low over the day bed. Inexpensive high tech furniture is both practical and stylish with co-ordinating fabrics in grey and pink and lots of cushions. An adequate number of power points means less unsightly trailing wires, while headphones preserve the peace.

them and then later on supply a lamp that can be angled directly on to whatever work is in progress.

If children are afraid of the dark but find that dimmed lights still give too much light, install a luminous plug in whatever outlet is best seen from the cot. They only consume one watt and yet that steady tiny glow can be comforting. It is worth noting, however, that there have been problems with luminous plugs and some are dangerous. There is no BS for them, so it is difficult for consumers to discriminate. Or put in the sort of miniature night light that only consumes a minimum amount of electricity.

Make sure that there is at least one

light switch that can be reached by even the smallest child.

For safety's sake

● Install all outlets well out of reach of toddlers — which means above skirting or baseboard height.

● Have existing outlets child-proofed or shuttered so that children cannot stick their fingers or toys (pencils, scissors and so on) in them.

● Keep any free-standing lights or appliances well out of reach of very young children.

● Avoid trailing wires or flexes. If you have a tv or stereo make sure they too are out of reach, and on a stable surface.

● Think about the effect of lighting on safety outside the room. Halls, corridors, staircases, kitchens and bathrooms are always potential accident spots in a home. (If you are not sure which parts of your home could be dangerous, walk through it unlit at dusk — taking due care yourself, of course. Remember that what seems safe to an adult might not be so for a small child. Make sure stairs and corridors are well lit at all times with light directed on the floor to show changes in levels or surfaces. You could install miniature (say four watt) night lights in all stair/landing areas plus one in the bathroom and these could be left on all night without costing too much.

Heating

Heating for a child's room should be even and not too hot, 18–21°C (65–70°F) is ideal.

If you have no central heating, thermostatically controlled electric storage heaters or radiators are a good idea. Any electric fires should be wall-mounted and well out of reach of children.

If you are installing heating, you should, as in all other rooms, place the radiators near the areas of greatest heat loss, that is under the windows. Individually thermostatically controlled radiators that you can turn up when the child is bathed (ideally newborn babies need a room temperature of 27°C/80°F, when being bathed) and make cooler for sleeping are a good idea.

Remember that it is illegal to leave a child under twelve in a room with an unguarded fire. Fireguards should comply by law with BS 1945 and be fitted to all electric, gas or paraffin heaters. Free-standing, nursery-type fireguards, such as you would put round an open fire, should comply to BS 3140.

Heat loss from fireplaces, windows, doors should be remedied by chimney throats, and strips of draught excluder. Do make sure that you are not eliminating all the fresh air, however: it is essential to be able to open the windows and bricked in fireplaces should be vented with an airbrick.

For the first few years of children's lives their own room (with the exception, perhaps, of the kitchen) is virtually their whole world. So, when it comes to designing any sort of space for them, the aim should be to create a warm and welcoming environment in which they can grow and develop and open up their senses.

For some people this is a signal to try and create rooms that are as full of fantasy and fun and humour as possible. But it is advisable, economically and psychologically to go for a purely temporary fantasy effect that can be changed to make quite a different sort of room as the child grows older. You cannot, after all, sleep in a train-shaped bed or underneath a castle headboard for ever.

The same applies to the actual arrangement of the space in the room. When children are very small you can divide the space up in a way which might not work nearly so well once they grow older and taller. Then their needs will dictate quite a different sort of division. In addition, you have to realize, as one architect put it 'that children naturally tend to create chaos and you have to learn to strike a balance between what they do and what you can live with'.

Obviously not many families can afford to change their children's rooms around very often, hence the wisdom of the staged plan for the sensible basic room in the first chapter, but they can certainly change arrangements and emphasis within the room, and most easily of all, they can change the colours.

The two things that all child psychologists seem to agree on are the importance of a child's first environment and the fact that all small children respond to and are stimulated by colour. Infants also respond well to movement (they love watching mobiles above a cot), to noises (bells and musical box devices strung across the pram), to shapes, textures and smells, but colour is far and away the most important stimulus. Fortunately it is the easiest and most economical way to transform a room completely. Use this chapter and Walls and Ceilings (pages 51–61) for ideas.

Clever use of blue and white and a kite-shaped light peps up a box-like room for very little cost (left), while a sturdy play-frame and platform system with toughened glass windows turn a bedroom into an adventure playground (right).

DECORATING IDEAS

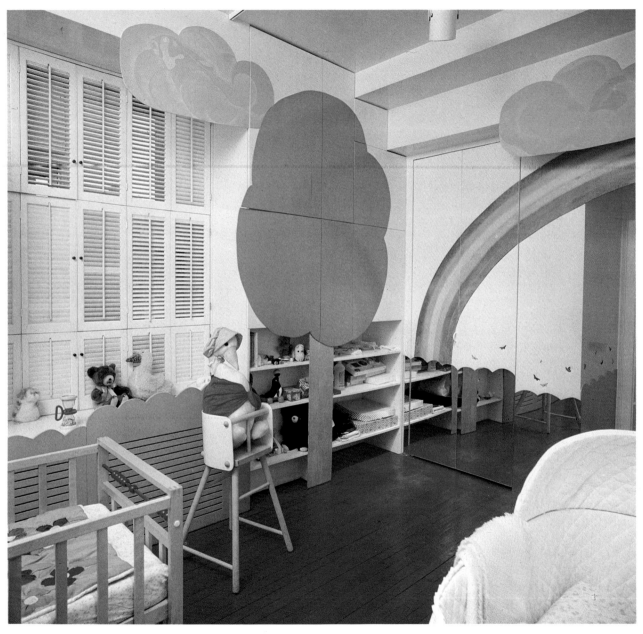

How to use colour

Once the framework of a child's room is settled, the inside can be altered at will simply by wielding a paint brush, pasting on paper, changing the window or bed treatments or, for that matter, applying paint-on or paste-up supergraphics like clouds, rainbows, butterflies, nursery rhyme characters, giant letters or numbers. Murals are only one step further on from this and the brave parent or willing artistic friend can transform walls, and thus rooms, into fairy-tale gardens, circuses, cowboy prairies, forests or whatever takes their fancy.

Quite apart from the many and varied decorative uses of colour in treating walls, floors, ceilings, furniture and windows, colour can also be used to form demarcation areas. It can be a purely visual way of dividing two sleeping areas or private play territories or marking off sleeping from play space simply by painting relevant parts of the floor or walls in different shades.

Colour used on walls can be put there to serve as a rich and varied background to set off other colours

Left: A fantasy room uses simple plywood cut-outs to make effective trees, hedges, rainbow and clouds, with the first two masking pragmatic storage. The bright red painted floor adds warmth; the mirrored wardrobe doors, more space and light.

in the room or it can be injected in vivid accents against an all-white, easy-to-clean form of decoration.

Colour can transform old furniture to make it work as part of a scheme. Or, if you have more than one child sharing a room, paint each child's own particular furniture a different colour. This colour zoning can also be applied to individual drawers in a shared chest, or shelves in a bookcase unit, or cupboard fronts. Even if the colour is just applied to the handles, it is enough to identify it to the owner of the space. This is a very good and easy way to encourage tidiness and respect for other people's possessions from a very early age.

Remember that paints used for children's furniture and equipment should be non-toxic.

How to use space

When we think of space we tend to think only of floor space and therefore miss many of its other exciting possibilities. There's an awful lot of unused space in every room and one way of bringing it into play in a child's room is to build in different

Right: A bedroom takes on a new dimension when the bed is a double decker London bus complete with wheels and plausible graphics. A wooden ladder leads to the play area on the top deck. Note too, vividly lacquered walls, ceiling and floor.

DECORATING IDEAS

levels so that the space can be divided neatly for various activities.

You can build platforms making wide steps that use the available space twice over or you can elaborate on the bunk bed idea. There are endless ingenious variations you can achieve here using plywood sides cut into different shapes. You can take off into the realms of fantasy: for instance, with bunk beds turned into a double-decker London Transport bus; or a farmyard barn with 'windows' cut out of the uprights and the top bunk covered with a 'roof' complete with dormer window; or two-tiered space capsules (with the help of old sonotubes — those fibre moulds used for making concrete pillars and available from large building sites); or Punch and Judy-like theatres; or stables; a ship's cabin complete with portholes; forts and towers.

Or you can construct something along the lines of the playhouse/ climbing-frame structures which combine sleeping, work, storage and exercise areas within one sturdy, workaday unit. It can include all sorts of parallel bars, swings, slides, steps, trapezes, ropes, balconies, mattresses, work surfaces, cupboard

A nursery looks especially pretty decorated in sugar almond colours: pink, blue and yellow (left). Old chests of drawers can be cheaply painted to match walls and fabric.

space, shelves and closets – a really intensive use of the space available.

On a simpler level there are the portable platforms of different sizes which can be placed together like huge steps. These have to be on castors so that they can be reasonably easily moved around. One large wide platform becomes the bed and cube-like structures behind it act as bedhead and extra storage as well as steps to open shelving behind.

The extra advantage of all these structures is that, once they have served their purpose, they can be dismantled leaving the essential ingredients like beds, shelves and so on to be re-situated separately somewhere else in the room, perhaps under a different or more conventional guise. While the framework of the room remains quite untouched, it will now have gained some space for more ordinary or classic furnishings.

The platform structures can also, of course, be moved from house to house if the family moves, or be re-used somewhere else for subsequent children.

More fantastic ideas

The sort of island unit fantasies that can be made out of bunk beds, plywood and a good deal of ingenuity are one way of putting a lot of fun into a child's room, but it is possible to make fantasy rooms

Let your imagination run riot and come up with a wide range of colourful ideas: a bed can become a racing car (above left), parked outside a playhouse which doubles as storage unit. Staggered bunk beds (left) feature a proper staircase dwarfed by a giant pinboard. Or integrate special storage for small toys and a seating area below (above) into a corner to leave the floor relatively free for playing. Sturdy ladder and balcony rails are essential for safety

DECORATING IDEAS

simply by decorating the walls, ceilings and floors.

A New York designer who specializes in children's rooms, developed a series of fantastic ideas for his son's room. When the boy was a toddler, his room was the end of the rainbow, with the rainbow painted on the wall and plywood cut-out clouds suspended from the ceiling to float above him (see page 30). Plywood was cut in the shape of trees and hedges, with the whole scene reflected in plastic mirror. Now, somewhat older, the child has a completely different room, fully wired for electronic hook-up to the family's central audio-visual system. It is also multi-levelled, with lots of built-in furniture in natural wood and practical plastic laminated tops, ceramic tiles, and only an authentic suit of armour adds a touch of fantasy. Yet another idea is to create a farmyard (see far right). A high-level bed is a sleeping loft, reached by a ladder, with an attached slide for quick exit. This sleeping loft rests partly on an old chest of drawers painted into the design and partly on hollow storage/play space.

To divide up the room a little as well as to make the yard more realistic, the designer built a shallow platform just beside the barn with its own real post-and-rail fence. He covered this raised area in an old remnant of green carpet to make it

look like a field and covered the 'earth' beneath it with another remnant of old brown carpet. A black and white vinyl cow lying sleepily in 'the grass' made a tolerably comfortable sofa, walls were painted sky blue with sun and occasional clouds, and a pair of plastic geese lights looked thoroughly realistic in the setting.

The effect of both these fantasy rooms was totally beguiling and enormous fun yet they were capable of being turned back into more everyday rooms when the time came.

Involving your children

As children grow up, encourage them to take an interest in design and in their environment by involving them when you need to redecorate their room.

Use their hobbies or particular passions of the moment (computer games, pop stars, collecting foreign souvenirs) as starting points for decorative schemes. For fun, paper the walls with posters or charts (one wall or a chimney breast may be enough): the sky at night for budding astronomers; cars for motor fanatics; wild flower identity pictures for naturalists. Add other decorative touches to fit in with the hobby: luminous stars to shine on the ceiling; a racing track painted on to the floor for cars; pictures from pressed flowers. Aviation enthusiasts may want to convert their

By rights, children should be encouraged to express their own interests in the decoration of their rooms. The colourful hang-gliding paper (opposite page) has been used as the starting point for a striking blue-and-white room which includes some interesting ideas for storage.

Woodland folk theme linen (left) for a younger child has been elaborated into a mural on the wall and over the handy storage shelves. This makes the most of a small room. Motor fanatics will love the racing car bed and petrol pump mural (above left). Or create a farmyard atmosphere (above) with a mock-barn sleeping area, green grass carpet and a swing.

35

beds to aeroplanes – tongue-and-groove boarding can cheaply convert one end of the bed while plywood cut out and attached to two bedside tables could make the wings.

Older children can have more say in the matter. Even if their ideas are bolder, weirder or more adventurous than you bargained for, let them have their head if you can bear it. Provide some basics like flooring and a bed, and let them do some of the choosing of extra accessories and colours. Never mind if they come up with an all-purple room; they're the ones who have to live with it, not you. Discuss cost with them and point out that they must be able to restore the room to its original condition if necessary (when you move, for example), since their choice may not be to other people's taste.

Today's children are certain to want some very expensive items among their equipment: record players, radios, tvs, computers. Unless you have a lot of money to spare, or have existing but dated equipment which can be relegated from a family living room to make way for more up-to-date versions, it is always sensible to discuss the acquisition of such goods with your children and how these things are to be paid for. If children are aware of the cost of decorations and furnishings they are more likely to treat them with greater respect.

Recreate a traditional but practical nursery atmosphere. The room (left) features an old-fashioned painted brass bed, draped curtains, frilled cushions and lace tablecloth; paint and stencils on furniture (above) echo the colour and design of the smocked curtains.

How practical is nostalgia?

If you feel strongly that an experience you enjoyed as a child or something you remember affectionately would be a good thing to hand on to your children, then why not try to re-create it? You may find, however, that some aspects of the old-fashioned nursery are quite impractical today, while others either still work amazingly well or have been brought up to date without losing their intrinsic charm.

For example, nursery fires and a club fender were fine in the days of vigilant nannies and willing housemaids, but even the substitute gas log or coal fires, while pretty, trouble-free and effective, need just as much guarding when children are around. Not easy for mothers without help.

A good many of the frills and furbelows of lace and muslin that frothed around Victorian cribs are seldom good washing-machine fodder today; they needed to be hand-washed, starched and crisply ironed for maximum effect. On the other hand, there are excellent modern fabrics which look just as pretty and can be tossed into the washing-machine with impunity. Many of these good-looking, easy-care fabrics which have become available only in recent years are quite cap-

able, by virtue of their design, of creating their own nostalgic effect.

Some of the furniture and furnishings one connects with nice old-fashioned nurseries — the capacious stripped pine and painted pieces, the painted and stencilled floor boards, the charming wallpaper — are still often the best and most practical solutions for a real nursery, that is to say, a sleeping/play space for a pre-school-age child. However, the wallpaper might be made that much more practical and immune to fiddling little fingers if it is washable or given a couple of coats of clear polyurethane to protect its surface. And to make it still more impervious you could bring back another sensible old-fashioned idea — the dado. This can easily be done by running a piece of wooden moulding around the room at waist height and painting the wall below white so that any scribbles — and there are bound to be some — won't do much damage. The wallpaper is hung above the dado. It would be even more practical if you covered the area below the dado rail with

An Edwardian pine bed (left) has been made to look authentic with a lace bedcover, flounced tablecloths and matching bed valance – all available in today's easy-care fabrics. Lacy and frilled pillows, arrangements of dried flowers and flowery prints complete the effect.

37

DECORATING IDEAS

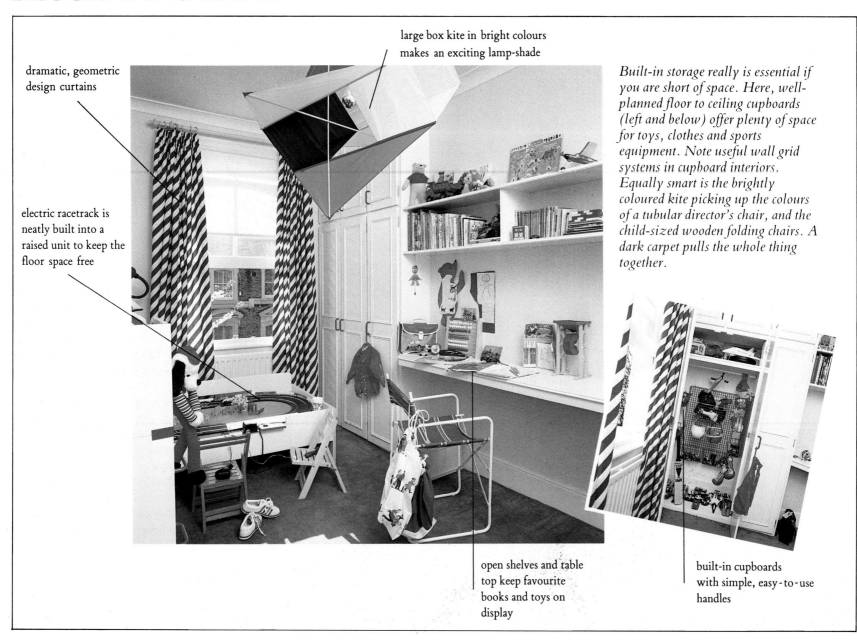

large box kite in bright colours makes an exciting lamp-shade

dramatic, geometric design curtains

electric racetrack is neatly built into a raised unit to keep the floor space free

Built-in storage really is essential if you are short of space. Here, well-planned floor to ceiling cupboards (left and below) offer plenty of space for toys, clothes and sports equipment. Note useful wall grid systems in cupboard interiors. Equally smart is the brightly coloured kite picking up the colours of a tubular director's chair, and the child-sized wooden folding chairs. A dark carpet pulls the whole thing together.

open shelves and table top keep favourite books and toys on display

built-in cupboards with simple, easy-to-use handles

Pure white with splashes of colour (right) looks very graphic. Walls and floor are easy-wipe to allow children to be artistic and still be practical. Sturdy card furniture is cheap but smart; felt pen scribbles on the walls can be wiped away. This is a fine system if your child realises that the rest of the house is not to be treated in the same way. The super bright room (below) has added rainbow colours to a basically white scheme with sturdy tubular and wood furniture. Cushions, blind and bedcover are a dazzle of rainbow colours with plenty of storage and play area built into the system.

removable blackboard or blackboard paint. There are dark green versions of both that are less oppressive than the conventional but heavy black. This way nostalgia is perfectly workable as long as you are sensible and selective.

Be thoroughly modern

The traditional look, with its old pine or painted furniture and practical prettiness, is one way of treating a child's room; at the other end of the decorating scale is the bang-up-to-date, streamlined modern look. And it isn't at all out of place because by modern I mean using the best of today's surfaces, furniture and equipment with a good deal of sleek but useful built-in furniture that can serve several purposes at once — like the sleep/work/play/storage units described earlier in the chapter. Thoroughly practical, easy-care, easy-clean from the parent's point of view, they are just as stimulating from the child's.

In the modern room the colours are generally bold or white with bright flashes of accent colour. Or the room can be all wood and cork. Or you could go for the best of both worlds with multi-purpose furniture and the latest in work surfaces with pretty and nostalgic touches in say the window treatments or wallpaper. As in all decoration, it is a question of taste and whatever suits your lifestyle and bank balance.

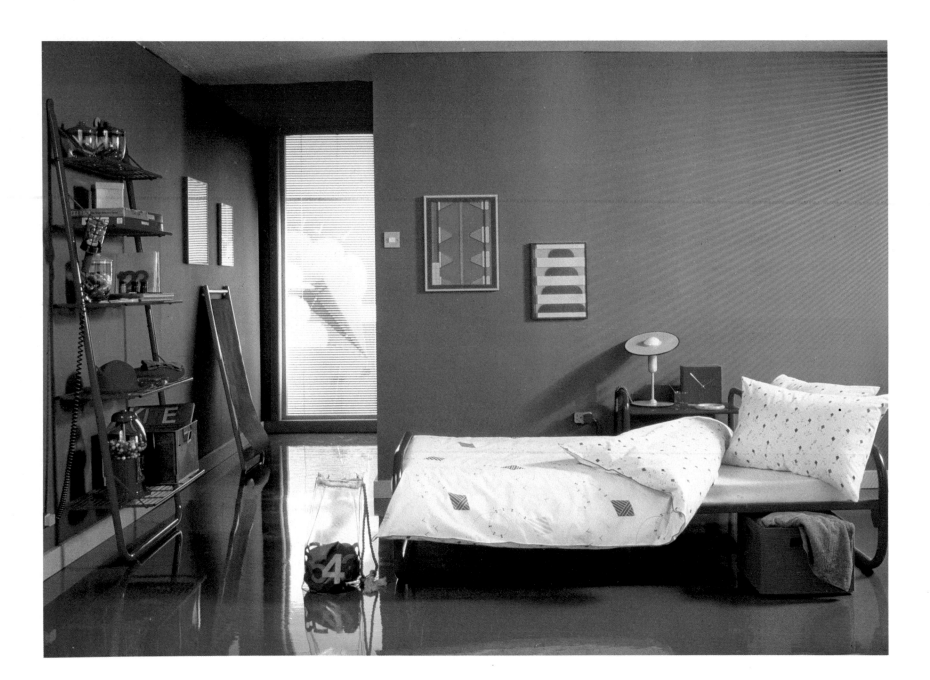

With decorating it makes sense to start with the floor. Once a child is out of the cot, the floor is his natural habitat. Children will happily gravitate there, disregarding all other seating and all other furniture. They lie on it, sit on it, crawl all over it, play on it, draw on it — it's their home. So it's important to make sure that in the early years at least, there's as much uncluttered space as possible and that it's a comfortable place to be. It follows that how you treat it and what covering you choose for it have to be the first and major considerations.

In any child's room the floor needs to be reasonably warm to the touch and free from draughts so that the baby/toddler can crawl about comfortably; it must be very easy to clean and maintain since spills and puddles are everyday occurrences; it should be as non-slip as possible and not too hard so that the inevitable falls and tumbles don't do any damage. At the same time it should be resilient, tough and as sound-proof as possible, especially if the room is not on the ground floor — the patter of tiny feet soon becomes a resounding thump. If the floor is also reasonably flat and smooth it will make a much better surface for children to play on.

Bearing all these requirements in mind you still have to make the basic choice between a hard floor and a soft one, but avoiding extremes in each case.

What are the choices?

Vinyl-coated cork tiles have a lot to recommend them: they are easy to clean, soft (as hard floors go), reasonably warm to the touch, tough, splinter-free and good-looking. Their natural tones would blend with any colour scheme. They are also economically priced and can be bought in suitably small quantities. *Vinyl tiles or sheet vinyls* are easy to wipe clean and hard-wearing but a little on the cold side. They come in a good range of plain colours.

Cushioned vinyl has all the virtues of vinyl plus softness.

Bright paint is a cheap way of transforming a room into something special (opposite). Deep blue for the walls, hard-wearing green gloss with several coats of polyurethane on the floor looks stunning. Ground floor bedroom (right) has floor-to-ceiling toughened glass to add safety to the feeling of space and light.

Linoleum is making a come-back and has lots of advantages. It is tremendously hard-wearing, tolerably soft, convenient to clean and can be cut into all sorts of shapes and designs. Its dull drab days are over and it is now being produced and used in very exciting patterns.

Polyurethaned wood looks handsome and can be wiped clean very easily but it must be made splinter-free. An old floor can, of course, be painted or painted and stencilled before being given several coats of polyurethane to make it thoroughly practical. Alternatively, farmyards or race tracks can be painted on the floor for fun. Bear in mind that floorboards, whatever the finish, will be noisier than other surfaces as there is no insulating layer.

Rubber stud flooring is soft and noise-resistant, easy to clean and available in good colours.

On the soft side

Carpet is certainly comfortable and noise-absorbing and can be either colourful in its own right or neutral to go with all the other colours in the room, but it isn't really very practical. It is, however, the best way to prevent sounds travelling to other rooms in the house and is good in apartment buildings. Stained carpet is not easy to clean although the new fibres like Enkalon are more resistant to dirt.

Any carpet should have a smooth

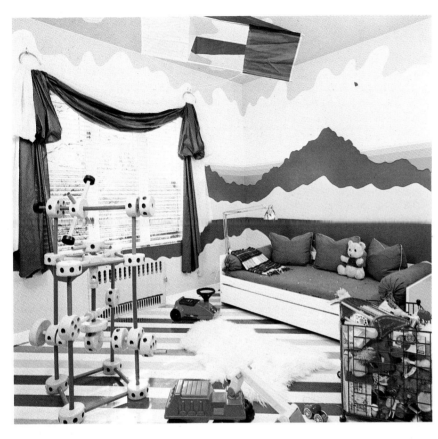

finish so that toys can be wheeled and pushed without coming to grief; do not use long or shag pile — it is too impractical.

Smooth-finish *carpet tiles* are a good idea because ruined or worn ones can be replaced at comparatively little expense. They are now available in a variety of finishes but all can be picked up individually and cleaned if necessary.

Wool/cord and hair cord and the *man-made fibre mixes* look neat and interesting but they are not very easy to clean; nor is their rather scratchy texture very comfortable for children when crawling or pushing toys.

Practical and fun

The best solution, according to child psychologists and infant school teachers, is to have a mixture of both hard and soft with islands of one or the other in the form of rugs, or different levels of carpeted platforms which can be used for various activities such as sitting, reading and playing. Their great practical and visual advantage is that they define areas and limits without forming any physical barriers. You can add to the island effect and achieve comfort by having lots of floor cushions on any hard floors; they make great playthings for small children and teenagers love lounging about on them too.

If you must have carpet you can always bring in vinyl or rubber mats to cater for any messy activities like working with modelling clay, painting, glueing and so on. Even large ones are quite light and can be easily moved away for cleaning or to another room or to the garden so that the child can play there and still have some temporary territory that he can call his own.

Alternatively, you can have half the room carpeted and the other half covered in vinyl or vinyl-coated cork or polyurethaned wood.

Floors with well defined areas looked at from a child's point of view, that is from a near-horizontal position, will appear like a large sea or lake with safe and accessible islands in it. Far more reassuring than a vast plain expanse.

Insulation

If you can afford it, it is a good idea to insulate floors. The benefits work in two ways. Hi-fi, tv or radio in a downstairs room is less likely to disturb children when they want to work or sleep and their daytime noises are less likely to be a nuisance to you. There are two things to remember about insulation: soft materials are better sound insulators than hard ones and the more layers on the floor, the better insulated it will be. If you are laying carpet, put down insulating board directly over the floorboards, then hardboard. A rubber underlay between the hard-

Left: Get the children to help you and create something like this zany paint-spattered and striped room (opposite) where bright colours, a slide and climbing frame and gay furniture instil instant liveliness. Note how stripes across the width of a wall-length Venetian blind have been cleverly extended with paint around one side of the room to end in great sploshes of colour with a matching pattern on the floor.

Above: The same colours are used in a more ambitious way in this fantasy room. The red, yellow and blue of a suspended box kite have been used to great effect on the walls, and in varnished stripes on the floor. Running the stripes diagonally across the room makes it look larger as do the generous swags of fabric hung at the window. A simple day bed and a wire trolley for toys leaves the floor free for play.

43

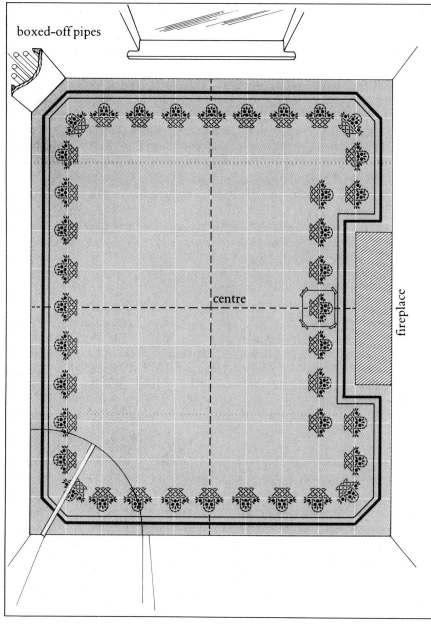

boxed-off pipes

centre

fireplace

Positioning a stencil border

To square off a floor for stencilling you need to take the measurements of the floor first and use them to draw a plan to scale on a sheet of squared paper. The floor drawn here is an average 4 × 3 metre (12 × 10 ft) room with boxed-off pipes in one corner and a fireplace. Measure your stencil block and decide on an appropriate scale. The size of the stencil block used here (see the photograph on page 47 for detail) was 20cm (8in) in diameter. As we wanted a 10cm (4in) space between each stencil we drew up our plan to a scale of 1 square = 30cm (1ft). Find and mark with chalk the centres of the walls and mark off the positions of the stencil pattern blocks, allowing for whatever space you choose between the wall and the stencil border. To take in the boxed-off pipes, we cut off the corner and repeated this device for decorative consistency in each of the other three corners.

If you want to add any stencils in the centre of the floor, you should stretch a piece of heavily chalked string between the centres of both pairs of opposite walls. Where the two lines cross will be the centre of the room. Working from the centre, position any additional stencils at equal distances away from it.

board and the carpet will act as a further insulating layer as well as saving wear on the carpet.

Lay insulating board and hardboard before laying vinyl, cork and tiled flooring. For an unusual but effective finish, lay sheets of chipboard over insulating board for extra insulation and varnish them; the result is similar to cork tiles. When sound waves travel from one room to another, one of the routes they take is through the unplastered portion of the wall under the floorboards. You can improve insulation here by removing the floorboards and rendering any bare bricks or building blocks and filling cracks round joists with ready mixed concrete mortar. Allow to dry out before replacing floorboards and laying your flooring finish.

The decorative floor

As the children grow older you can adapt the floor in various ways depending on what they need to keep them (and you) happy. If they are fairly rumbustious and noisy, the floor should obviously be as indestructible and sound-proof as possible. But it might well be that they would appreciate a rather decorative floor and this can be achieved by painting or stencilling. If you are at all handy and imaginative into the bargain, painting or stencilling a design or some sort of graphic effect can be a very rewarding exercise and

Floors should be hard-wearing and practical as well as looking good: plain boards (above left) have been sanded and varnished for a natural finish, while those in the loft room (far left) have been stained blue to match the beds. With more expensive floor coverings, make sure you pick one that can withstand the everyday wear and tear. Plain tiles (above) are smart and long lasting while the modern rubber stud floor (left) is sturdy.

not as difficult as you think. One idea, with practical as well as decorative qualities, is to paint or stencil board-games on to the floor. This could include a giant checkers board or perhaps a game of snakes and ladders. Use card to make outsize counters.

There are many ways of setting about it. If you are thinking say, of stencilling and you have a wood floor, it would be very effective to have the rest of the floor bleached first. Stencilling with darker stains over a lighter background can produce a very interesting looking finish.

How to bleach a floor

Bleached-out boards can look quite spectacular provided the surface has been sanded in the first place. Punch in any nails that may protrude with a nail punch. Hire a power sander (this looks like a cross between a mowing machine and an upright vacuum cleaner) from a tool hire shop. Finish the edges with a hand-held disc sander. Sometimes it is enough to scrub ordinary domestic bleach well in and then rinse off. If this does not seem particularly successful, try strong chemical bleach used with great care and according to the directions on the packet. Allow to dry thoroughly. Then give a sealing coat of polyurethane, plus a couple of further coats of varnish for additional protection.

Alternatively, and more professionally, you can lighten floors either by staining or by a paint-and-rub-off method.

Staining

First sand your floor. Then apply a white stain, thinned down by 50 per cent with mineral or white spirit, and spread it over the boards with a roller.

Wait a few seconds, then wipe it up with a clean cloth. Let the surface dry, then apply one coat of the following mixture: 5 per cent white stain mixed with 95 per cent matt polyurethane. Let this dry for 24 hours.

Then apply a second coat of polyurethane on its own. When it is dry, rub on two coats of ordinary white floor wax.

Paint-and-rub-off

Another way of achieving an interesting bleached effect is to apply white oil paint and then rub most of it off. The method is as follows:

Use flat white oil paint, slightly tinted, if you like, with artists' oil paint. Brush the paint over the wood, a small section at a time, and then rub it off against the grain. Do not be over-vigorous because the whole point is to leave some paint engrained in the cracks. If the floor is very gappy you can add a little spackle to the paint to thicken it up so that it will fill the crevices. The

surface will, however, need smoothing with sandpaper afterwards.

Once the paint is quite dry, you can repeat the process until you get the scrubbed-down, bleached-out look that is right for you. Give the surface a couple of coats of polyurethane applied as above.

Paint it

If floorboards are in too bad a condition to be revived by sanding and bleaching by either of the above methods, they might still be rescuable using solid paint which can cover a multitude of faults. After painting, the surface will have to be finished off with several coats of polyurethane and given a topping-up coat of polyurethane every year. Even so, painted floors can stand up to a surprising amount of wear and tear and the paint can be used to give all sorts of different effects.

You can, of course, paint over vinyl or linoleum, but if you want to stencil, it is probably better to cover the old floor with hardboard or plywood which you have first treated with primer.

Which paint to use?

Although deck or yacht paint is often sold specially for floors, you can use any of the following successfully, depending on what sort of finish and effect you require. It's essential to use an oil-based primer or undercoat first.

Cheap flooring ideas are usually ideal for children's rooms where they will take considerable punishment over a relatively short period of time. If you have the time and patience and you want a more decorative effect, bleaching the boards and stencilling in different colours can look stunning, especially if continued onto the walls or furniture to match. Red and green fruit design (below right) on cupboards has been used in a smaller, co-ordinating pattern on the floor and skirting boards. A couple of coats of polyurethane varnish will protect the design and can be re-applied when needed.

Heavy duty coir matting (above right) is strong, practical and inexpensive. Easy to lay in sections, it can be lifted for sweeping and cleaning and provides a warm, natural coloured background.

Sisal flooring (far right) creates much the same effect but is less bulky and can be bought by the square metre. Here it has been used to create a neutral, nicely-textured background for some strong shapes and colours. Chocolate brown wardrobe storage balances the glow of the natural pine furniture. Bright red accessories and a large pinboard of favourite pictures really bring the whole room alive.

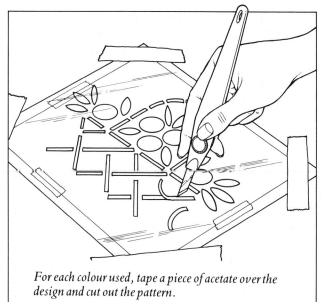

For each colour used, tape a piece of acetate over the design and cut out the pattern.

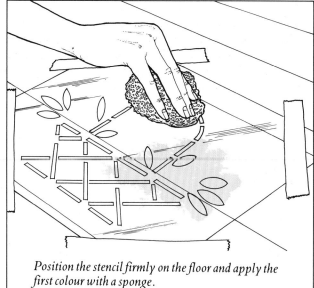

Position the stencil firmly on the floor and apply the first colour with a sponge.

After the paint has dried, add the other colours in turn using the same technique.

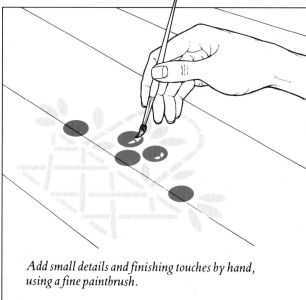

Add small details and finishing touches by hand, using a fine paintbrush.

Oil-based flat or eggshell paints make a good base for any decorative finish. *Enamel paints* give a hard durable finish but are more expensive and have a more solid appearance.
Casein paints are good and cheap but have a strong smell.
Artists' acrylic, Japan or Signwriters' colours — all obtainable from artists' supply shops — are expensive but good for stencilling.
Oil-based eggshell and gloss paints or epoxy paints are best for any previously tiled surface.

The important thing to remember when painting floors is that boards must first be given a couple of thin coats of undercoat and left to dry properly. To ensure an even finish, tint the undercoat with whatever colour the top coat is to be; in this way you should only need one top coat for a plain paint job.

How to stencil

If you want to try your hand at stencilling this is how to go about it.

You can use ready-made stencil kits from art shops and good stationers or you can buy printed sheets and then adapt and alter them. Or you can invent your own; taking inspiration from anywhere and everywhere, old pictures, fabrics, wallpapers, whatever design seems appropriate.

It's wise to experiment first either on sheets of paper or on a test area of floor (or wall). You'll soon discover that the ancient art of stencilling is a very useful one because it can bring decorative interest and individuality to a dull space and be continued on to walls, furniture and ceilings to give a unified look and theme to a room. In fact stencilling is a cheap, quite easy and very effective means of achieving almost instant transformations on any surface.

Make your own stencils

Before you start, you will need to assemble the following items:
Finecraft or Exacto knife and blades (from art supply or DIY stores)
Pencil
Paper for drawing your design on
Masking tape
Acetate sheets 0.05 (from good stationery and art shops)
Natural sponges cut into small pieces, or soft, stubby, natural bristle stencil brushes
Small detail brush
Plastic cups
Plastic bags
Artists' acrylic paints (from art supply shops)

Draw or trace your pattern or design on the paper. Until you get the hang of stencilling it's best to start with a simple design. If necessary use a photostat to blow a design you want to copy up to the size you require. Put a piece of acetate over the design and tape it firmly in place. Now cut out the pattern using the craft knife or Exacto blade. Don't lift the point of the blade as you cut; instead, turn the design slowly and this will ensure a smooth edge for your stencil. Use a different sheet of acetate for each colour, cutting out only the relevant elements of the design.

Now mix your paints in the plastic cups to whatever colours you want. Aim for a fairly thick consistency so that the paint won't run under the edges of the stencil.

Tape the acetate stencil to the floor. Dip a piece of sponge in paint and blot off any excess. Using a bouncing or up-and-down motion, apply paint to the floor through the stencil which then must be removed carefully from the surface. Repeat all round the room in one colour, then, when dry, add the other colours in turn. Small details can be added with a fine brush and minor errors touched over in the same way. As the acetate sheeting tends to wear out and also become clogged with paint, it's advisable to cut several stencils so that you go on getting a clear and definite line. It is no good trying to wash acetate; just throw it away. Stencilling is fairly finicky work and takes time, so in between sessions cover your paints with plastic bags.

Once you have gained confidence there'll be no stopping you and you'll want to stencil everything and achieve better and better decorative effects. You're not limited to the floor: furniture and even fabrics can be stencilled to match. The scope in a children's room is limitless. You can have supergraphics on the floor as well as on the walls and you can use stencils to make imaginative demarcation areas. These can be anything from grassy fields with flowers to maps, seashore, river-banks, jungles. It is all a question of practice, confidence and a free-ranging imagination.

As you become more proficient with the standard stencilling technique, you may wish to try something more elaborate, maybe extending it to items of furniture in the room. This tropical paradise (below) was created on a row of wardrobe doors using a wide range of colours and a variety of techniques including a soft, graduated colour effect. Quick-drying acrylics are perfect for a stencil of this scale as they are less likely to smudge or run.

The negative view of walls is to look on them as confining and restricting; in children's rooms the opposite should be true. Even when walls act as boundaries to a particular space they should seem to provide a sense of security and, later on, privacy. At the same time they have tremendous potential as areas of great visual interest and as such, a source of constant stimulation. Children start noticing them from the cradle so treat them as blank canvasses that can be adapted to all sorts of bright and exciting ideas that change, keep pace and grow up with the child.

Before you start decorating, decide whether the walls need insulating to prevent noisy children (and parents) from disturbing each other. The simplest way to insulate is to put up a second layer of plasterboard over the existing wall finish. For extra insulation, the new plasterboard should be mounted on battens away from the existing wall, and a layer of insulating material (like loft insulation) fixed between the old and new wall. You'll have to remove skirtings and electrical fittings before fitting the new plasterboard (see also note on rendering the wall beneath the floorboards, p.44).

Even a large noticeboard, made of insulation board and covered with felt, will cut down on reverberations in a room and help to insulate it to some extent.

Another alternative is to insulate the walls of a room adjoining a child's room. If your bedroom, for instance, is divided by a partition wall from your child's room, put insulation to work as a decorative finish by lining the walls of your room with polyester wadding, stapled in place, and covering it with stretched, pleated or gathered fabric, fixed to battens round the top and bottom of the wall.

Decoration

The most practical and economical start for children's walls is to paint them in white gloss which looks clean, can be kept fresh-looking with a quick wipe of a damp cloth, and which makes an excellent and durable background for anything that goes on it or against it. It also gives

Generous use of fabric for walls, windows and drapes (opposite) not only looks good but keeps out the draughts too. Clever painting can transform a plain two-door wardrobe into the semblance of a country cottage (right).

WALLS AND CEILINGS

you all the scope you need for choosing furniture and decorations that are as colourful as possible.

Gradually add storage units in fashionable pastels or bold primary colours or plain wood, as well as supergraphics, toys, cut-outs, prints, paintings (including the child's own efforts), books, kites, posters, pin-boards, photographs, whatever you, and later *they*, like. They will all look tremendously colourful against the white background. Everything can and will be changed around as the child grows older but all you need do is freshen the walls behind, either with a good wash down or another coat of white paint. It's an easy solution, the maintenance is negligible and everybody will be happy.

One very successful way of getting the best of both worlds is to run a dado or chair rail either all round the room or round one or two walls at waist height or slightly higher. It can be quite easily done by sticking up a length of wood moulding or simply by painting a horizontal stripe of colour. The object is to

Right: Try to consider children's favourite interests and possessions when planning their rooms. A keen reader has been provided with plenty of bookshelf space, plain sand walls for displaying colourful kites and friezes, a dramatic midnight blue ceiling and a smart dado.

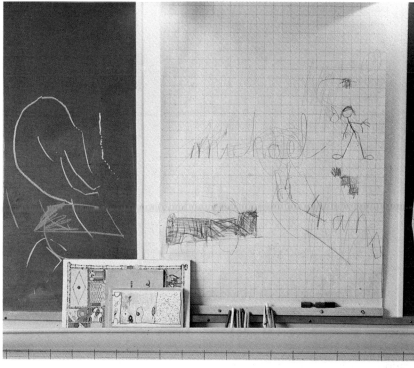

give you an upper and a lower wall which can each be given a different decorative treatment. And since children are incorrigible scribblers and chalkers, you'll save yourself a lot of trouble by providing them with an outlet for all their mural activity in the form of a blackboard on the lower part of the wall.

Or make the dado into a frieze of cut-outs of every shape and sort, put together like one of those Victorian scrap-screens and then varnished over. I remember as a child being endlessly fascinated by just such a dado in a friend's house. It was always being changed and added to and I loved it.

To achieve something along the same lines more easily, cover the dado in scenic or pictorial wall-paper. There is a paper on the market which is just right for the job; a jungly-animal design which is only partially coloured. The children are free to do the rest and each roll comes complete with a bundle of coloured crayons. Again, do remind them that the freedom to scrawl on walls does not extend beyond the limitations of their rooms.

Try a mixture of all these ideas to keep the children interested or ring the changes as and when you want to. One easy way of achieving this is to make the whole dado of pin-board or chipboard which can be bought in any timber yard, then painted.

A dado doesn't have to be for ever. When its day is done and its usefulness outlived, the blackboard, the wood moulding and the pin-board can all be taken down to make way for new wall treatments.

A white painted wood-panelled dado (above left) visually straightens an awkwardly-shaped room under the eaves and provides a wipe-down surface for sticky fingers. The area can be safely wallpapered to hide any irregularities in the walls and sloped ceiling. Discourage scribbling on the walls with an area set aside for the purpose at comfortable child level. An area for pictures and doodles (above) can be combined with a blackboard or pinboard and a handy tray for pens, chalks and crayons.

Often your imagination can be triggered by a feature of the room, a poster or favourite toy, and extended quite cheaply using paint, fabric and paper cut-outs to make an exciting colourful setting. A sloped roof (left) has been cleverly transformed into a painted red and white awning. With bright blue walls, matching blind and a border of stencilled flowers, the room has a cheery toy-town atmosphere.

Similarly a giant poster (above) tails off onto the ceiling with large painted stars. The rest of the room is kept a sensible plain white to act as a calming influence.

White is always a good foil for dazzling primaries as well as being easy to clean and touch up. Solid blocks of colour (above right) are sharpened and lifted by white wood-work, ceiling and piano, while simple coloured stencils (right) have been used to brighten a striped wall.

Bright ideas for bold walls
- Huge oversize posters in stunning colours for say, circuses or cars, used like wallpaper on one wall or over cupboards and overlapping on to the ceiling.
- A 'hedge' of green-painted cork stuck on to cut-out plywood panels (in hedge shapes) around the bed area of a room.
- A frieze of toadstools, grasses, flowers, insects, either painted straight on to the walls or cut out of coloured papers and stuck on. Either way they can be removed quite easily when children outgrow them.
- Large cut-out letters of the alphabet or numbers pasted on to the walls.
- Groups of twelve birds or butterflies or animals for easy counting lessons.
- A blown-up map varnished over to cover one whole wall.
- Flowing supergraphics (lines, circles, shapes of all kinds) to help define private or separate areas in a shared room.
- A dark green gloss wall in an otherwise white room for throwing soft balls against.
- A New York or London skyline at skirting board level with cloud-dotted blue skies on the walls, for older children. A night-time version could be achieved with a black silhouette and stars on a deep blue background.

55

WALLS AND CEILINGS

Make way for art

You have to be realistic about children. It is absolutely no good expecting them to keep their rooms immaculate or to imagine for one minute that they are going to stay quiet and well-behaved inside a little showcase. What you can try to do is to make them aware that they can do more or less what they like in their own space but not in yours, and then to see that all surfaces in that space are as tough and easily cleanable as possible. There are bound to be marks and scuffs and scribbles and the best way is to face the fact and deal with them on the 'if-you-can't-beat-them-join-them' principle. This is where you can make a virtue out of necessity. Children generally love drawing and all sorts of artistic self-expression, and to them, walls must seem a marvellous natural canvas. So build on that. Bring the two together deliberately by giving them an actual wall or part of a wall to experiment – and daub to their heart's content. This will give them more space and scope than even the blackboard dado but in any case, if you have determined scribblers or Picassos in the making, they would overflow from the blackboard. For the time being you'll just have to close your eyes to conventionality, give them the freedom to express themselves over a large area and take heart from the knowledge that

you can paint or paper it all over later when the scribbling phase is over.

If you cannot bear to see your walls treated like this or you live in rented accommodation, pin up large sheets of paper which can be exchanged for fresh pieces when necessary. Nobody wants to destroy artistic urges but it's better for everybody's sanity to channel them where they can do no harm and to let children understand clearly what is allowed and where. So do stress that this freedom should *not* be extended elsewhere in the home, much less in other people's houses.

Practical or pretty?

If your taste, or that of your child's is for rather prettier decorative effects, one way of achieving this is by using attractive wallpapers. By choosing carefully, it's possible to achieve the prettiness without sacrificing any of the practical advantage of paint.

Look for papers that are washable or wipeable — even scrubbable — tough enough to withstand the onslaught of grubby and fiddly little fingers but still able to act as a good background for accumulated pictures and objects rather than be the main decoration in their own right. Unless of course you can afford the luxury of regular change or a separate bedroom that doesn't have to double as playspace.

Above: With today's wide choice of easy-care co-ordinated ranges, you can choose a scheme that is pretty as well as practical. Cool blue has been used on the walls and mock dado of this nursery and matched with a cot cover and comfy cushion for the nursing chair. The use of wood and blue and yellow accessories adds contrast and a natural warmth.

Right: Blue looks equally good used in conjunction with white and touches of bright red. Pale blue painted trim and chest look fresh and pin neat against a white sprigged paper and dramatic red furniture. Cork tiles on the back of the door make a great space-saving pinboard and there is plenty of room for study, entertaining and sleeping.

If a paper takes your fancy but isn't wipeable or washable you can usually make it stronger and easy to clean by giving it an overcoat or two of matt polyurethane. This has the effect of yellowing most papers a little so you must bear this in mind; also check first that the colours will not run. Do this by applying the polyurethane over just one corner or strip. If you are going to give more than one coat you must let the first coat dry for a full 24 hours before you put on the next, otherwise you will get a rather sticky mess.

Two into one will go

Most children actually prefer quite small spaces: they seem more secure and cosy, they are more manageable and more private. Even an average-sized room must appear vast to a tiny child, so it's quite possible to divide such rooms into two, either to make room for another child or to provide separate sleeping and play areas.

Room dividers can come in a multitude of shapes, forms and materials. You can make them of plywood, wallboard or plaster board; you can have half walls or whole walls and you can cut through them with all sorts of shapes from conventional arches to circles, semi-circles and slits. One good idea is to use a wall of blackboard on castors so it can be moved

space-saving bookshelves are
handy for storing bed-time books

a disused fireplace
is transformed into a
self-contained play area

bunk beds tucked
neatly into the alcove
leave the floor free
for play

trompe l'oeil
portholes add a note of
fun by the bedside

pull-out colour-coded
crates under the bed provide
valuable extra storage for
clothes and toys

*Rooms are rarely perfect – the secret is to
make them work for you like this exciting
room, where bunk beds and bookshelves are
effectively fitted into an alcove, and a
disused fireplace becomes a magical doorway
to a Moorish castle. Plain, deep yellow
walls provide an excellent foil for colourful
objects. A renovated card index file is ideal
for storing small toys.*

Right: Careful planning means one room can cleverly sleep two teenage girls by partially dividing it with a double desk unit and co-ordinating curtains on an ingenious system of lightweight metal rails. Matching beds incorporate handy drawers for storage and double as sofas during the daytime.

to one side of the room or the other — or away altogether. Or, for fun, how about a divider wall crenellated like a castle, with toys perched in between the crenellations? On one side you could have a cot and play-space for a toddler, on the other, bunk beds and storage for an older child.

Children love tiers and towers and enjoy climbing and clambering up and around them so why not an actual tower structure built from a series of tall plywood panels with curved tops, tall enough to take a couple of bunk beds. One of the panels could take a long curved corner-window complete with a curtain, the other might perhaps have two 'portholes' and a third could support a brightly-painted ladder for reaching the top bunk.

It is essential that such ingenious shapes and devices allow both 'rooms' to benefit from the light from the window and let you look through from one area to the next. In this way even a limited space will never seem cramped.

You do not need to be particularly artistic to create fanciful pictures on your walls like these. Use bought stencils and transfers; or trace off your favourite cartoon and nursery rhyme characters, transfer them onto the wall and let your children help you colour them in with quick-drying, wipeable artist's acrylic paints. Even the smallest detail will brighten a corner, like the amusing mousehole (above). This room includes a whole storybook of charming characters cleverly added to the natural features of the building. A sloping ceiling has been transformed into a magical skylight with moon, stars, hey diddle diddle favourites and Rupert Bear dropping in for a visit by balloon. A painted pie on the mantlepiece has released the traditional two dozen blackbirds and Polly Flinders offers a cup of tea by the fire-side.

Even the door can take on a new dimension when Little Bo Peep decides to drop by (right) complete with Mary's little lamb and Jack and Jill. This combination of trompe l'oeil and bright cartoon characters is remarkably effective in a plain painted room. Remember that children are only a couple of feet tall and place your murals accordingly: here Humpty Dumpty is about to fall off a low wall below an elaborate hickory dickory clock complete with mice. The same room even includes a large, low trompe l'oeil window (above) revealing a fantasy landscape with Little Red Riding Hood and the Owl and the Pussycat. Colourful murals such as these can be made more durable with a quick coat of matt or satin polyurethane varnish which will enable sticky fingerprints to be wiped off at the end of the day.

Dividers in children's rooms must be securely fixed: they will be 'charged' by toys on wheels and made a target for climbing activities. This should be borne in mind when designing them. Either make them low, solid and easy to clamber over, or upright, secure and sheer – not a temptation for young budding mountaineers.

Ceilings — a chance for fantasy

In a child's room the ceiling can provide an opportunity for indulging in fantasy. You can paint it with clouds or circles like portholes; you can add birds, butterflies, aeroplanes, even footprints. The whole area could be a map, real or imaginary or even, for aspiring astronomers, the sky at night, full of stars and planets. And then, of course, you can create another dimension by hanging things from the ceiling — mobiles, kites, model aircraft, punch balls, flags.

The whole feeling of the space of a room can be subtly altered by painting banks of colour up the walls, over the ceiling and down the other side again, or by sticking paper friezes all round the walls just below the ceiling and edging on to it. Even if you leave the walls plain you can wallpaper the ceiling with a decorative scene or geometric design, confident that it's safe from sticky fingers up there.

61

The main consideration about windows in a child's room, apart from seeing that they provide enough daylight and fresh air, is that they should be safe. Even quite young children can be dangerously adventurous and agile climbers.

If windows are set low enough on a wall for a child to be tempted to climb out of them you will certainly need to put up some sort of temporary screen or bars which can be fixed to a frame set into the window. Horizontal bars tend to be an aid and invitation to further climbing, so vertical ones are better; see that they're spaced so that a child cannot get his head stuck between them. If you think they look too prison-like, you can always paint them different colours to cheer them up.

From the safety aspect, they should be made of safe non-toxic material and leave a gap of not less than 60mm (2½ in) and not more than 85mm (3½ in) between adjacent vertical bars. Moreover, they should be removable in the event of fire, ideally fitted with childproof locks.

Practical possibilities

It is not usually a good idea to put long curtains in a child's room. They can too easily be tugged at and pulled down when the child is crawling, or tripped over and generally in the way. If you really want curtains, it is best to keep them short. A double row of café curtains would be both neat and attractive.

On the whole, blinds of one sort or another are a more satisfactory solution for various reasons. They're safe, easier to clean than curtains and control the light more efficiently. Black-out shades are practical since they can be pulled right up to let in maximum light and air or be pulled down to darken the room totally. With any luck this will delay the start of the day for you when the children are very young by ensuring that they don't wake at the first sign of morning light. Also, if you want them to sleep in the middle of the day it's a great help to have a darkened room, particularly on bright summer days when curtains are rarely adequate.

Blinds are not only practical they come in a wide range of colours and designs which always look striking, like the red, yellow and blue ones (opposite). Traditional pink patterned bedroom (right) has a matching fabric blind and pelmet.

Don't forget windows are useful areas for built-under storage, window seats and toy chests, and should be fitted with safety bars, grids, or child-proof locks if the child is at risk of climbing up and falling out. Storage units under the large blue painted windows (far left) incorporate shelves, cupboards and drawers that have been painted to match the windows and child-sized furniture. A compact room within a room has been created (top left) by building the bed under the window and screening with frilled pelmets and generous curtains. Bookshelves behind and ample storage above and below make a virtually self-contained bedroom, for an older child, within a remarkably small area. The interestingly timber-framed window (below left) manages to incorporate a matching play platform, continuing the line of the raised fireplace and at the same time providing storage for toys below. Removable bannister rails make decorative window bars.

Right: A striking blind can easily provide the focal point for a room and an inspiration for the rest of the scheme. A white slatted blind with vivid red, yellow and green stripe effect has been copied in the rest of the room with clean white fitted furniture and bright red and yellow accessories against a strong blue spotted wallpaper.

Special effects

A bedroom fit for the proverbial
princess has been achieved here
simply with colour and inexpensive
fabric. The window was the starting
point and was swathed in deep rose
curtains, draped beneath a rose-
painted pelmet and held aside with
matching tie-backs. An equally
luxurious-looking rose-pink
patterned fabric was used both for a
festoon blind and the long curtains
round the bed. The bed curtains
were lined with the same plain pink
as the window fabric and hung from
a rail concealed behind the pelmet
and attached to the ceiling over the
bed area. In this way a simple divan
has been given all the grandeur of a
four poster. The pelmet has also
been painted pink and decorated
with a co-ordinating pink-sprigged
border which is continued all round
the room. The useful vanitory unit
with its louvred doors is pine
stained with a mahogany varnish to
match the mirror above and the
small elegant desk. The final
touches are provided by the much
darker rose of the carpet which
matches the lamp bases, the
inexpensive round table covered
with a floor length cloth in the same
fabric as the bed curtains, a
matching cushion, and neat pink
and white candy striped pillows and
bed valence. All of these effects have
been achieved by using good
quality, but reasonably priced,
fabrics, and visual effects, such as a
mahogany varnish, rather than
expensive furnishings.

If you want something that performs the same function but looks more decorative, you can have ordinary roller blinds with blackout backings. Or there are cloth blinds or shades of various designs with silver backings. These are specially useful because they have insulating properties which help prevent heat loss in winter and act as heat reflectors in summer.

Vinyl-coated blinds or shades are practical because they can be wiped clean with a damp cloth or sponge. Venetian blinds are helpful because they allow you to control the light so well — useful for daytime rests and in the summer. They come plain or coloured or in a rainbow of colours and can be ordered in all the shades of one colour, for example from palest pink through to deep rose or burgundy.

If windows are a major feature, make the most of them with clever window dressing, like this room (left) which has three to deal with. Walls have sensibly been painted plain white and the windows emphasised with dramatic red gloss paint. Floor length red and white check gingham curtains hung from red painted poles are edged in a matching large check and co-ordinated with patchwork cushions. Red and white ceiling light and red painted beams reinforce the impact created by the curtains.

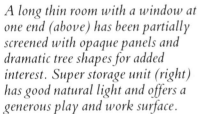

A long thin room with a window at one end (above) has been partially screened with opaque panels and dramatic tree shapes for added interest. Super storage unit (right) has good natural light and offers a generous play and work surface.

Slatted wood blinds are handsome, look specially nice in an older child's room and will control the light well. Inexpensive pinoleum or matchstick or bamboo slatted blinds filter the light to a certain extent but won't keep it out altogether.

Vertical blinds look good and neat and they, too, come in white or a wide choice of colours.

If you do decide to put up blinds at the windows, it might also be worth considering using matching ones, instead of more expensive doors, to conceal clothes, shelves and even beds.

A word of caution if you use blinds of any sort. Do make sure that you can keep the cords well out of reach of toddlers and crawlers who like to grab everything in sight. Cords can be a potentially lethal hazard if the child gets entangled in them, quite apart from ruining the blind's mechanism if they are mishandled.

If you buy white or pastel roller blinds they can be used like a canvas to paint designs on. You can also use wooden blinds and pinoleum or matchstick blinds in this way if you spray them white first.

Window frames too, can be used as part of the decoration. Painted in brilliant colours, yellow, blue, red, green, they look marvellous against white walls. And if you hang things from the pelmets, like birdcages, or kites, you get a wonderful decorative effect when the sun shines through them.

The nice thing about windows is that they are virtually as versatile as the walls. You can keep them as plain and functional or as decorative and functional as you like. They can be changed quite easily and at little expense as the child grows older.

Very few children are born tidy. That's worth remembering. However, though a sense of order is not something that comes naturally to them, oddly enough they do enjoy convenience. So organize storage as conveniently as you can for, in the end, it will benefit you as much as them.

You only have to watch a child rummaging impatiently in a deep drawer for a favourite thing and chucking everything else out in an unruly heap as he tries to find it, to see that stacks of drawers are not necessarily the answer to organization, at least not for toys, and not in the early stages.

The great thing is not to give children an excuse for untidiness. Make it easy to be tidy and make it fun. When they're very small the best way is to store possessions other than clothes in places where they can see and reach them. Low shelves, rows of cubby holes, bins, baskets, trays, low hooks, are all helpful and practical. If you can get children into the habit of *knowing* they will find a particular item in a particular place, they might be persuaded to put it back there for the next time.

Madame Montessori, who started the famous nursery school system, always said that everything that went together should go on some sort of tray; children can then just pull out the right tray and find what they want at once. This way everything is easy to find and easy to put back. The same method can apply even to clothes. Small children's clothes are not bulky and can be folded on to a tray and put away on shelves. Low-sided wicker trays, rather like those flattish baskets used in offices as in-and-out letter trays are good and inexpensive. Rectangular shapes are better than round ones, and you make the best possible use of space if they all fit neatly on to shelves.

Clever containers

In fact, you can glean a whole lot of useful ideas by looking at office and even kitchen equipment to see what you can usefully borrow, copy or improvise. Those stacking perspex containers or stacking shallow drawers are ideal for children's

Good storage is essential to keeping children's rooms tidy. Whether it is achieved by buying customized furniture, like the well-planned wood-veneered range, left, or of a more improvised nature, right, is a question of money and taste.

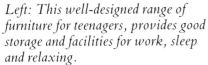

Left: This well-designed range of furniture for teenagers, provides good storage and facilities for work, sleep and relaxing.

Above: Redundant wooden fruit and vegetable containers make attractive as well as inexpensive forms of storage.

Above right: Fruit containers are used here not for toys but shoes, which like the clothes hung on a low rail below the shelf, are easily accessible to the independent child.

Right: Intriguing paper and rafia containers, decorative as well as practical, are ideal for storing small treasures.

storage: everything is visible and they also come in bright colours. Brand new plastic dustbins can make practical containers for toys.

Again, taking a leaf out of nursery and infant school practice, it is a good idea to make even better use of colour by using it as an essential part of a storage system. If you use large coloured cube containers, all red things can go in a red cube, yellow in a yellow one and so on.

It helps too, to organize things by size. It doesn't do to have, say, crayons, paints, pencils, small toys and so on put side by side with large toys where they get lost or broken. Give small objects their own small containers.

It is an expensive luxury to buy special, small-sized, easy-to-reach storage. Even with several children in mind it'll soon be outgrown and need replacing in no time at all. Better to buy full-size items straight off or improvise until you can afford them. Wooden crates from your local greengrocer, or those tough, round cardboard bins from wallpaper or fabric shops all make sturdy containers, ideal for toy storage. Paint them in vivid colours and fix wheels or castors to them, not just for easy mobility but so that they become playthings in their own right as well. Children are always enthusiastic about anything they can pull around and pretend is something else: a house, a ship, a car, even a horse.

73

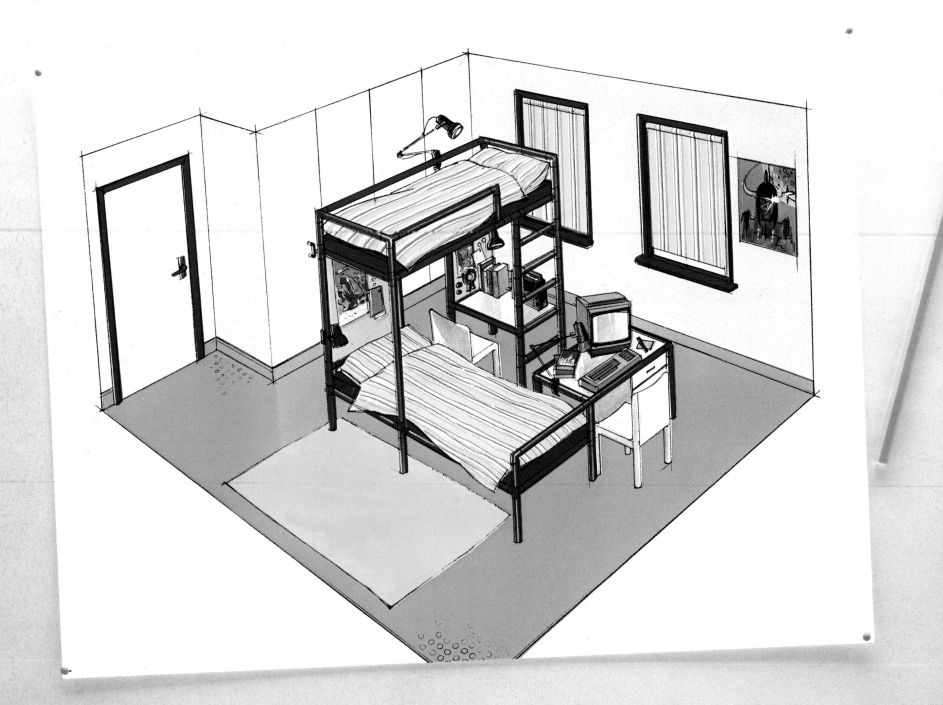

Room for one more

Built-in cupboards and modular
sleep and study units mean you can
fit all the features you need into
minimum space. This room has
made maximum use of a bright red
scaffolding system to build an island
unit which features two bunk beds,
twin study areas, lighting and even
ample pin-board space, leaving the
walls free for a run of built-in
wardrobes in plain white to provide
useful but unobtrusive storage for
clothes. The scaffolding system is
ideal for multi-purpose rooms such
as these since it can be dismantled
and re-assembled with very little
bother to suit changing needs. Here
it has been used to create L-shaped
bunk beds with integral desk units
at right angles, perfect for reading,
study, mini-computer and cassette
radio. Positionable spot-lights have
been included in the system so
lighting is good and there is plenty
of pin-board space, attached to the
top bunk. The chosen colour
scheme is fresh and cheerful: red
painted door and window frames to
match the scaffolding, a hard-
wearing green rubber studded floor
and a yellow non-slip woven rug.
All these colours are picked up in a
bright striped fabric for duvet
covers and blinds, with a plain red
fabric for the fitted mattress covers.
Both are easy-care and easy-clean:
duvets make bed-making simple
and less of a chore, blinds are cleaner
and far more practical than curtains.

ALL IMPORTANT STORAGE

platform provides additional
storage and play area

wall light illuminates
platform area

pale blue walls visually
enlarge space

*No space has been wasted in this
well-thought-out and compact room.
A platform provides additional
storage and a play area, with a
wardrobe slotted in beneath the steps.
The pale blue painted walls help to
enlarge the room visually and
provide a good foil to the yellow and
red accessories. Although the
dimensions of this room are minimal,
there is ample space for play, work
and sleep.*

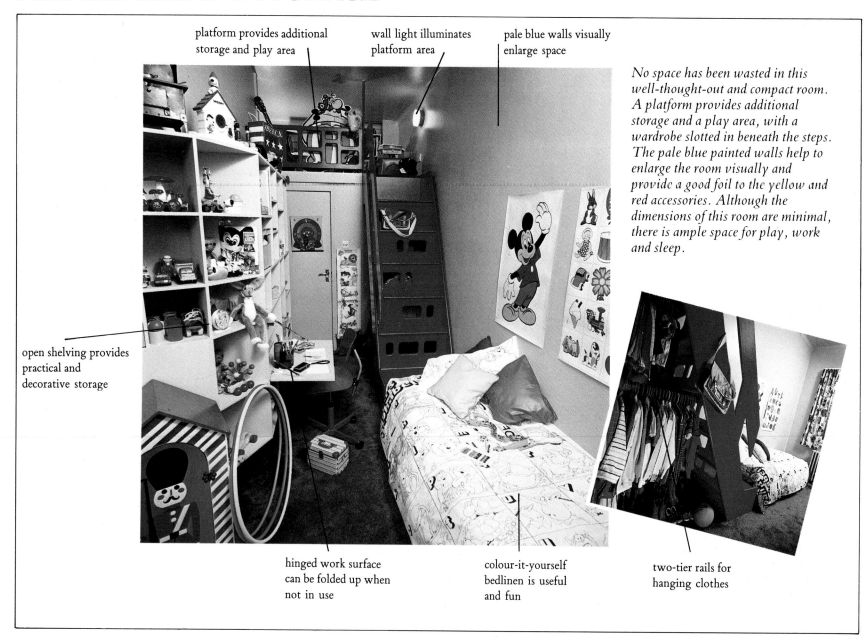

open shelving provides
practical and
decorative storage

hinged work surface
can be folded up when
not in use

colour-it-yourself
bedlinen is useful
and fun

two-tier rails for
hanging clothes

Waste paper and rubbish bins, the larger the better, and especially if they are light, plastic and brightly coloured, are great toy containers. So are stacking wire baskets, vegetable racks, laundry baskets, gym lockers or the kinds of lockers used for storing luggage on stations. These will hold everything down to shoes and sports stuff. They don't have to be gloomy grey or khaki. It's an easy matter to paint or spray them any colour you like to match the rest of the room. Later on they make useful wardrobes.

As the child gets older and taller you could also use filing cabinets. It's not such a good idea for small children who could easily pull them over on top of themselves or try to climb up them, but at the homework stage, a row of filing cabinets with a continuous top of wood or Formica and enough kneehole space to sit at, can provide both desk/play surface and storage combined. Buy them, preferably second-hand, with different sized drawers to take both small and large objects and paint them to suit the room.

Right: Well-planned work-cum-playrooms can stop you going up the wall. Flexible shelving units can be adapted to suit the individual needs of each child. These provide a desk-top, cork notice-board and storage for books and toys, and look good with the parallel bars set next door.

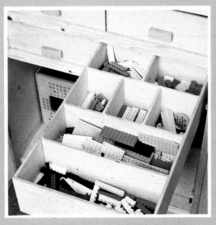

Versatile storage that works easily for the child may help discourage untidiness. Above left: These cleverly planned shelves not only provide a good means of storing small objects like cars, but are a toy in themselves. A road system has been painted on to the top shelf, while ramps provide access to 'roads' on other levels.

Above right: This sophisticated industrial shelving is tough, self-supporting and extremely versatile.

It will store clothes on rails, books and smaller possessions in jolly-coloured boxes, and fit into more or less any decorating scheme. Left and far left: Wood, whether painted or varnished, always looks good. This particular unit has been tailor-made to the requirements of the child concerned and even the drawers themselves (see detail photograph) have been compartmentalized to make finding possessions easier.

From kids' stuff to teenage clobber

It is important to choose storage that can change its role as the children grow older and their possessions change in size and quantity. When they are tiny you will need space to store nappies, small amounts of clothes (even large amounts of baby clothes don't take up much space), ointments, lotions, and so on; later the same space will take toys and odds and ends, and later still be used for books, models, electronic equipment, clothes and sports gear.

Trolleys or cots on wheels are particularly useful because they can take on a number of different roles, including that of plaything, over the years. Stacking boxes and cubes can be used in all sorts of configurations and their tops made to serve as work/play surfaces. If you decide on a shelving system, make sure the shelves are adjustable and as useful for small children as for teenagers. Units that have horizontal shelves and vertical divisions as well as integral cubes, drawers and even cupboards are marvellously useful because one way and another they will hold everything from books, records and toys to tapes, clothes and pictures. They will still look neat and tidy — even decorative. Since each thing is given its own particular area, it looks well organized — not just a jumble of possessions. If you can get such units on castors

they can also be used as room dividers. There are some kinds you can take apart to break up a large system into small units temporarily, using some, say by a child's bed, others all along a wall at waist level. Later they can all be put together in a floor to ceiling stack for a more sophisticated-looking arrangement.

Industrial shelving, that came into its own with the High-Tech look, has many good points to recommend it. Originally designed for factories, hospitals, restaurants, even greenhouses, it will take almost everything you can think of from folded clothes, shoes, sports equipment to rows of colourful containers for smaller objects.

Storage that's fun

Children's rooms offer the greatest scope for witty, clever, colourful ideas that can even make the serious

When two children share a room you can't afford to waste space. The mattress of each sofa bed rests on a bank of drawers which also serve as low tables at one end. A curtain acts as a room divider for one half of the room while a floor-to-ceiling tower of shelving, to which desks are attached, forms the remainder. The curtain can be drawn during the day to give the room a lighter, airier feeling. The curtains at the end of each bed conceal large closets for storing and hanging clothes.

ALL IMPORTANT STORAGE

business of being tidy and methodical more like an enjoyable game. Take a perfectly ordinary series of shelves. They may be essential to the room but rather boring. What can you do to liven them up? You could fix cup hooks on to the edges and hang nets or baskets from them for smaller temporary objects like balls, shuttlecocks, draughts, marbles, crayons

Ordinary whitewood or unpainted wood units are not expensive and can be painted in all sorts of decorative ways: all over, in stripes or different blocks of colour — a different colour for each drawer. Wardrobes can be divided into several levels for a small child and gradually emptied out so they are left for normal clothes use or removed so that hanging space grows with the child. The outside can be painted or covered to look an amusing part of the room. Where every inch of space is at a premium don't forget that the insides of wardrobe doors can be used. Fit them with white or coloured plastic coated grids with shelves and you have a whole new stacking place for odds and ends which otherwise might be all over the floor.

There are endless opportunities to be ingenious and imaginative and the more possibilities you can squeeze into whatever storage you decide on, the happier you and your children will be.

Left: These brightly coloured bunk-beds incorporate a wardrobe which also acts as a support. The large cardboard containers can be part of a game themselves or used to tidy away toys. The primary-coloured theme of the furniture is extended to the walls and soft furnishings.

Above: Making a virtue out of necessity — these old fruit and wicker baskets have been painted to give them fresh life as attractive containers for small objects.

Right: Kitchen-style sliding shelves make excellent use of an awkwardly-shaped but well-designed room.

On the whole, and unless money is no object, special child-sized mini furniture is rarely a good long term investment. It is all too soon outgrown and discarded and generally lacks the solidity and staying power that large and well-used pieces like tables and desks need.

Nevertheless, there are obviously certain pieces that really have to be made especially for infants and pre-school children: cradles, cribs and cots, high chairs and first chairs. The last-named often become some of the most prized of juvenile antiques and are handed down in families. As for the rest, the essential criteria for choosing and buying should be safety, sturdiness and practicality first and then, if possible, an element of fun. With regard to safety, there are government regulations for the flammability of upholstered furniture. Testing is carried out in accordance with BS 5852.

Because the choice is often overwhelming for first-time parents, it's best to make things a little simpler by thinking of such furniture in terms of activities and under such heads as furniture for sleeping, for sitting, for eating, playing, washing and for travelling.

Furniture for sleeping

Newborn babies don't care where they sleep as long as they are warm and well-protected in conditions emulating their mother's womb, particularly when she was walking and moving. What else could account for the popularity of the cradle with its ability to be gently rocked? This and the Moses basket have barely changed in design for centuries.

Of course it can be argued that cradles and cribs are an unnecessary extravagance since they are grown out of so quickly. Their advantages are that for a tiny baby they are snug and can be easily moved and carried around. In any event they can usually be borrowed from some other member of the family or from friends or passed on to others so that they serve their purpose many times over. On the negative side, the BSI do not encourage the use of items

Contrasting styles: The high-tech room on the left shows the sort of furniture which easily adapts to a growing child. The prettily furnished nursery, right, centres on a crib, which will obviously have to be replaced by a bed later on.

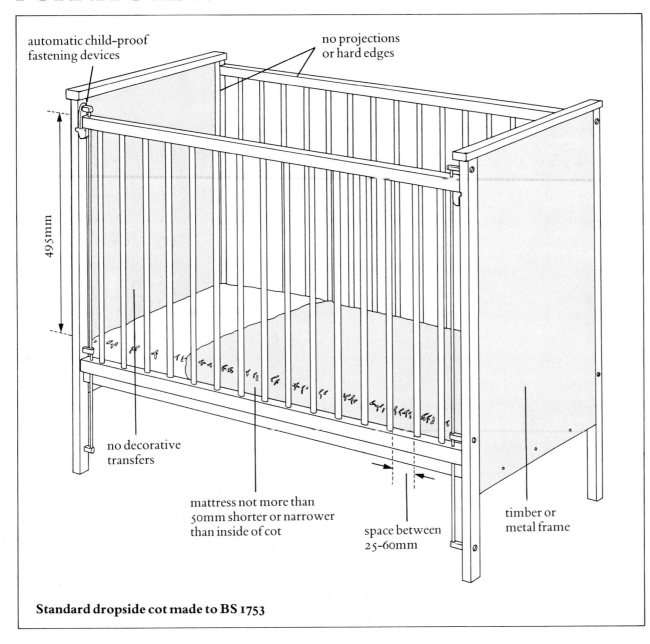

automatic child-proof
fastening devices

no projections
or hard edges

495mm

no decorative
transfers

mattress not more than
50mm shorter or narrower
than inside of cot

space between
25-60mm

timber or
metal frame

Standard dropside cot made to BS 1753

such as cribs, baskets or cradles. There are no standards for them and they are often made to intricate designs with little regard for safety.

Alternatively, you could just as easily use a carry cot for the first few months, or use the pram itself as a cradle, or a rigid Moses basket with a stand or even a converted laundry basket, box or drawer lined and suitably — ie not too softly — mattressed.

Buy a purpose-designed foam mattress – firm with a non-airtight cover. There are generally holes or pockets cut into the foam for extra safety. If you can't find one to fit exactly, buy a longer one and cut it down to size.

Carry cot

Most parents who intend to be at all mobile with their babies will want to buy a carry cot. These are the most important points to look for:
● The handles should be positioned to ensure a safe and steady ride whether one or two people are carrying it.
● If the cot can be collapsed into several parts it should be so designed that when set up again it cannot be accidentally dislodged.
● The cot should be made from harmless materials with no sharp edges or jagged bits anywhere.
● Both cot and stand should be strong and firm, and the stand should be rustproof.

• If the carry cot is going into a car it should be securely attached with harnesses but on no account should these be used to restrain the baby in the cot. There should be a separate harness for that attached to the cot's sides for use when travelling.

Cot

As the child gets older and more active and begins to be more aware of his or her surroundings, you will need to invest in a cot. Apart from minor variations in wood (there are also more costly polished steel versions) and a choice of slatted (preferable) or solid sides, most cots will look alike to the uninitiated. However there are differences and it is important to examine any cot you are thinking of buying with the most stringent safety aspects in mind.

The British and the American Federal Standards Institutes have issued the following directives both on the framework and the bedding; always look for them.

• The cot must be solidly constructed with no projections or exposed sharp edges on which babies could hurt themselves or snag their clothing.

Clever planning right from the start pays off as children's needs alter. Bunk beds make a safe place to rest a crib and will accommodate two children later on.

FURNITURE WITH A FUTURE

- The sides and edges of the cot must be high enough to stop a baby climbing out and have no horizontal bars or ledges to aid the act of climbing. They must also have adequate rail heights even when the dropside is lowered.
- The bar or slat spacing must be small enough (60mm/2⅜ in apart) to prevent a baby slipping, feet first, through the bars.
- If there is a dropside guide system, that fastening device should engage automatically so that babies cannot lower the sides on their own.
- Paintwork and materials must not be harmful to babies even if they suck or chew the cot. There should be no transfers on the inside.
- Cots should be made in standard sizes to fit standard mattresses and each cot should have a label letting you know which size mattress to use to ensure that there is enough room for bedclothes to be tucked in without leaving a dangerous gap, and that it is not thick enough to allow a baby to climb over the cot side.
- Mattresses should not have any handles (as adult mattresses do to facilitate turning) in which babies can get their arms and legs trapped.
- Both PVC-coated and spring interior mattresses should have at least four securely fixed ventilators in the sides or ends. It is also advisable to use an absorbent sheet on top in case of vomiting or wetting.

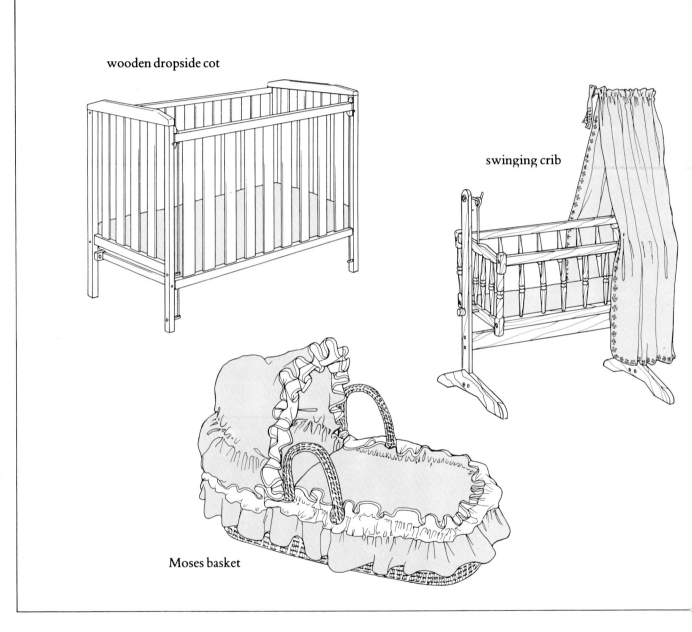

wooden dropside cot

swinging crib

Moses basket

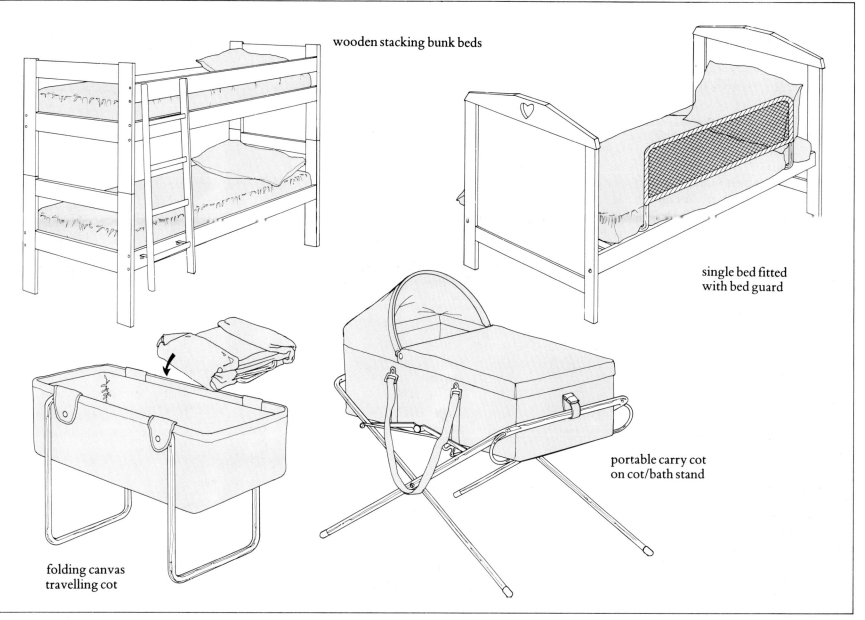

wooden stacking bunk beds

single bed fitted
with bed guard

portable carry cot
on cot/bath stand

folding canvas
travelling cot

- The fillings should be clean and harmless and only non-poisonous dyes and colours should be used.
- There should be a label telling you which size of cot the mattress should fit.
- Pillows should not be used until after the first birthday and any baby's pillow should carry a warning notice to this effect.
- The pillow and cover should be so designed to ensure that babies can still breathe properly when they are lying on their sides or fronts.
- The pillow should be firm enough to stop a baby's head sinking into it.
- Pillows should always be kept clean and dry. Cotton covers are best since they will allow adequate airflow, but they must fit tightly over the pillow so that there is no possibility of babies sucking any extra loose material into their mouths.
- Always take off and dispose of plastic covers from mattresses and pillows after buying them.

Beds

At an even later stage, the cot can give way to a bed. If you have more than one child, or your child wants friends to stay, and there is limited space, think of investing in a truckle bed (a bed which can be concealed under another bed). Other good space-savers are beds with drawers underneath for clothes, blankets and linen or toys. There are extravagant

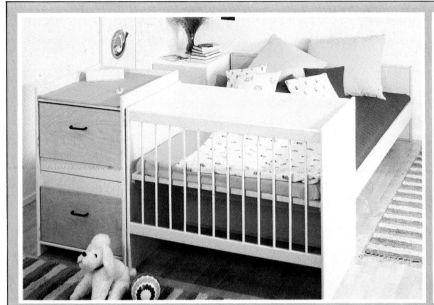

The hard-wearing shelving and storage units in these photographs will look just as good in a teenager's pad as in a baby's or toddler's room. The cot arrangement, top left, is built to convert into a bed, and the deep-drawered cabinet, which now provides a surface on which to change the baby and storage will also have a long life. The white cupboards and shelves, above and bottom left, provide a practical work surface, which with the addition of suitable chairs, lamps and mirrors can become desks, bookshelves or even a dressing table as required.

beds — extravagant because they will only be useful for limited periods — in the shape of cars or trains or boats. 'Junior' beds are also available, which are conventional in design but smaller than the standard single. They are equally extravagant in their way, as they are not large enough for adult use and children quickly grow out of them. And finally, there are the best playthings of all, adult-sized bunk beds which are as good for one as for two. These too, come in a variety of shapes and sizes and can be incorporated into elaborate climbing systems, tower structures and various fantasy creations (see chapter 2). But even the simplest models are good on all kinds of counts quite apart from the exercise, space-saving qualities and the security they provide for the child tucked in on the lower level who feels in a special little world.

The top level can be turned into another private area for reading or playing. Add book racks, lots of cushions, decorate that particular bit of ceiling with a map of the world (good for geography) or the night sky (good for astronomy) or, if the

Beds double as playthings when children can climb up to them and turn them into secret hideaways. Here, a roller blind effectively screens off the sleeping area. A second bed could be added later.

FURNITURE WITH A FUTURE

ceiling is very high, fix another 'roof', a suspended fabric canopy or a piece of wood on supports above. You can add roller blinds to the sides to give privacy, or more cheaply, pin on sheets which can be pulled aside like curtains.

Some models have drawers or shelves underneath for extra storage and there is a particularly useful kind that comes apart into separate beds for later on. Some even take apart to make good-looking sofas and are thus an excellent investment if you are intent on long-term planning (see chapter 1).

All bunks should have some sort of guard rails when children are young and it is not a good idea, of course, to put anyone less than five years old on the upper level. Check that the ladder has smooth slats and can be firmly or permanently fixed.

It is possible to buy adult-sized beds which have protective sides to them that can later be removed, or you can improvise your own.

A distinctly nautical feel has been given to this room by covering the walls and ceiling in white-painted wooden slats to create a cabin effect. A blue-and-white folding captain's chair picks out the tiny blue print of the bunk, cushions and Roman blinds. The bed easily becomes a daytime sofa, and model ships, wheel barometer, rope ladder and globe are clever finishing touches.

wall paintings reflect dominant
decorating colours

gloss-painted walls are
easy to keep clean

wardrobe doors and
handles integrated into
colour scheme

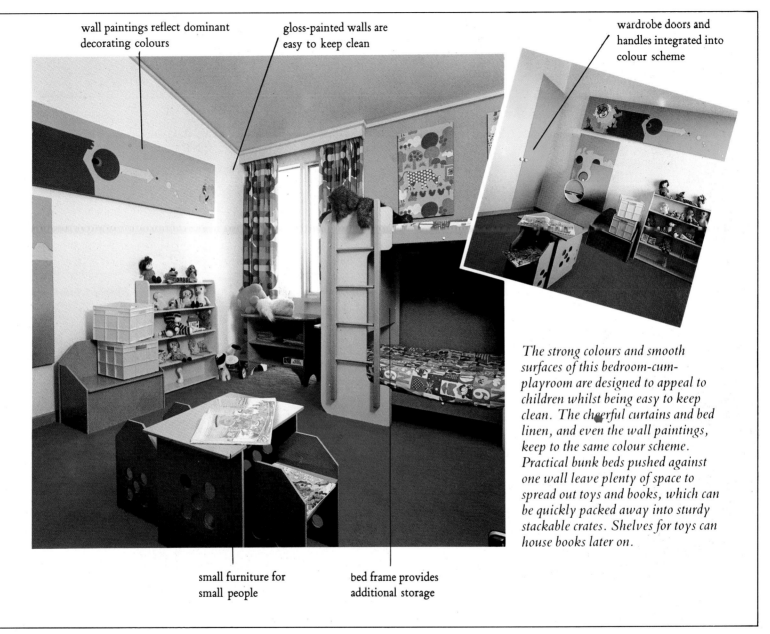

The strong colours and smooth surfaces of this bedroom-cum-playroom are designed to appeal to children whilst being easy to keep clean. The cheerful curtains and bed linen, and even the wall paintings, keep to the same colour scheme. Practical bunk beds pushed against one wall leave plenty of space to spread out toys and books, which can be quickly packed away into sturdy stackable crates. Shelves for toys can house books later on.

small furniture for
small people

bed frame provides
additional storage

Bedlinen

The essential factors to remember when choosing bedlinen for cots and children's beds is that it should be comfortable and practical for the child, hard-wearing and easy to clean for you. Luckily today's fibres mixing both natural and synthetic fabrics combine the best of both worlds, and come in an increasing selection of designs to suit every taste, style and pocket.

Duvets really have revolutionized bedmaking in the last ten years and are now available in cot and pram sizes. They are ideal for children, being light enough to allow freedom of movement and very warm as they settle to the natural shape of the body. They are generally available in different tog ratings: the higher the tog the warmer and lighter the duvet. There is a choice of fillings, all of which are machine washable: pure down is the lightest and warmest – and the most expensive; a mixture of feather and down is a good mid-range duvet, and there is synthetic filling – ideal for children with asthma or allergies and who will also need a foam pillow rather than feather.

Left: Bed linen in bright primary colours is a focal point in this modern bedroom. Carpet, blinds and chairs are kept plain, whilst the geometric pattern of the linen is echoed by the accessories.

Very different effects can be achieved by choosing fabrics carefully. Left: Pink furniture and rug form a plain background for the eye-catching picture-printed bedspread and curtains. The story-book theme is continued in the posters. Below right: A room fit for a princess. The four-poster bed, draped in a mauve flower print and a white lace bedspread, could be straight out of a fairy tale. Matching curtains and lampshade and lots of co-ordinating cushions add a luxurious touch. Below left: A light-hearted idea for bed-time. This washable colour-in duvet cover is printed with an animal alphabet and comes complete with a set of crayons.

Sensible seating for children. Top left: This sturdy chair and table set, ideal for playing, reading and eating on, has no sharp corners on which children could knock themselves. The chair has arms and a footrest for extra safety and is padded comfortably. Above: The same pieces of furniture are shown here made up into a highchair for meal times. The table becomes a wide base onto which the chair is firmly fixed. Left: Older children appreciate having extra chairs in their rooms for friends. They don't need to be expensive – bright, colourful deck-chairs would do nicely.

Furniture for sitting

Given the way most children prefer to sit on the floor anyway, you would think there was little need for chairs at an early age. In fact there are quite a number of chairs associated with each of a child's growing stages and all of which are very necessary to them.

In the beginning you need a good comfortable chair for nursing and feeding the baby. This should be low with either no arms at all or the sort that will allow the mother plenty of unrestricted movement. An ordinary straight-backed wooden kitchen chair with the legs shortened is ideal, padded out with cushions for comfort. Out of the baby stage you need the sort of relaxed chair that is both good for comfort and comforting and for climbing on: a capacious, overstuffed armchair with lavish arms that will go on to be a favourite chair for a child to curl up in to read. Children love being nursed and cuddled in a rocking chair and the smaller versions are comforting for small children to sit in while they watch a new baby being fed. If there isn't a spare knee to sit on, a rocking chair is a good place to be for watching television or listening to a story.

You will definitely need a strong, stable highchair, preferably one that can be adjusted to a convenient height for feeding the child from the table, or that can come apart to be put on a lower level. Unless you are fortunate enough to have a nursery, this will, of course, be located in the dining room or kitchen. There are low level chairs with trays as well, but a dual-purpose one will save money and space. If the chair is made of metal, there should be no sharp ends or open-ended tubes and when the feeding tray is in position there should be no possibility of the child slipping out from under it. There should also be a safety strap, a seat adjustment device that locks securely and, for maximum stability, the base should always be wider than the seat. You may have to buy the harness separately. Either way, make sure that there is firmly fixed anchorage for it. A proper foot rest adds comfort. As they get older children will need proper chairs so that they can sit at a table to eat, sturdy chairs to climb on to reach things, soft, comforting body-moulding chairs for relaxing in and chairs that give good support for working. They particularly like chairs that move (rockers, chairs on wheels or castors) or chairs that they can sink into, like bean bags or sag-bags. These should have fire-

A raised study area has been cleverly fitted into an awkward corner in this young girl's room. Pale lilac wooden furniture complements the wallpaper and makes the room especially feminine.

95

Left and above: The sofa bed is an extremely versatile piece of furniture which is capable of turning a bedroom (above) into a teenage bedsit (left) in a matter of minutes, and is particularly useful for children who want to entertain their friends in their own rooms and need privacy. The striped wallpaper and bed linen in the same room are in bright fresh colours to accentuate the non-bedroom feel.

retardant stuffing. Toddlers prefer low seats so that their legs rest on the floor, otherwise they get very tired. Stackable plastic chairs in bright colours are ideal for mealtimes and for working. So are sturdy wooden chairs, especially those with arms which feel safe and are more restful. Stools, too, are quite good for painting, model-building, drawing; there is an adjustable variety which will grow with the child. If you can get a step-stool you will find it invaluable in the bathroom (for reaching the basin or sink) as well as in their playrooms and/or bedrooms. Look for the kind with suction devices that keep them steady and firm.

Benches, wood-topped or upholstered are useful for accommodating several children, marvellous for games of pretend, especially as they can be turned upside down, good for putting under a window (with bars!) and handy for model-building when things can be spread out along them. From the safety point of view, there are not too many *don'ts* about chairs that are not taken care of by common sense but here are some points to bear in mind:
• Buy strong sturdy chairs that won't tip over when they are climbed on.
• Don't provide children under eight years old with canvas folding chairs as they could collapse when climbed on.
• Be wary of plastic or wood folding chairs. They might be sturdy enough but the folding mechanism could easily trap and hurt small fingers.
• Make sure wooden chairs are smooth and splinter free.
• Check that paint is non-toxic.

Furniture for playing and working

One of the biggest mistakes parents make when choosing furniture for children's rooms is to forget what it is like to be only a metre (3 feet) tall. Children need chairs and tables and surfaces they can relate to and it is easier for them to be comfortable with their feet on the floor.

If you have the space, a large low table with a wide horizontal surface is ideal for painting and drawing, especially if its legs are adjustable so that very small children can sit around it on the floor. Later it can be used as a desk, and if it is really quite large, for two desks divided down the middle with some sort of wooden or plastic pole or divider. If space is very tight, look for a collapsible table or one that folds down from the wall. It's useful to have this sort of spare table so that children impatient to get on with their own activities don't have to wait till you've cleared the kitchen or dining table.

Try to provide some sort of work surface as soon as the child starts school so he or she will automatically start doing projects and homework on that and not on the floor. If you can find a desk or surface with sides or can nestle it away in some alcove, say between bookshelves or cupboards, so much the better; children like a sense of being enclosed when they are concentrating and

Space has been found in this narrow room for a fair-sized desk alongside the convertible sofa. In this position it has good natural light during the day and for after dark there is a small lamp which is conveniently positioned for reading in bed. Wide shelves are useful for holding toys and books, while a white pinboard provides display space for favourite paintings and even dolls, and gives a much needed horizontal emphasis.

such a space will be different or seem different from the play space around them.

Blackboards, pin or tack boards and easels should all be part of a playroom's furniture, for children need vertical as well as horizontal surfaces. Boards on wheels are ideal

FURNITURE WITH A FUTURE

because they can also act as space dividers and the bigger the work space you can devote to covering with pin or tack board material like cork, felt-covered masonite or plaster board, the better.

Bulletin boards with brightly-coloured backgrounds are excellent for pinning up drawings, paintings, homework, pieces of first writing and so on. They could also make good headboards for beds.

Furniture for travelling

If you want to be at all mobile you will need to invest in a carry cot, preferably with a wheel base or transporter so that it can act as a temporary pram, or for that matter do instead of a pram. You may also need a pushchair or stroller, a portable high chair, a car seat and a baby carrier.

Carry cots Obviously if you are going to use your carry cot every day you will need to buy a better quality model than one just for temporary use and occasional car outings. In fact, if you have stairs or steps to negotiate before you can get into your house or flat, an easily detachable carry cot and transporter is a far better choice than a heavy pram.

Even more useful is a 'pram buggy'. A good model is made up of three parts: a transporter, carry cot and buggy seat. The transporter and

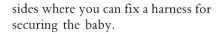

Left: This high-ceilinged room has been brought down to a level more manageable for children by painting the lower half of the walls with a bold blue wave motif. Yellow canvas blinds and roomy built-in wardrobe, red chairs, bed and door splash vividly against this background. Two wide, well-lit desks have been provided for homework.

Below: This folding blackboard fulfils various functions. As well as providing an indestructible surface for drawing and practising writing, it can also act as a room divider, or as a screen behind which general clutter can be stashed away.

carry cot can be used together as a pram and later, when the baby is older, the carry cot can be removed and the buggy seat attached. Some models come with a shopping tray and are even better value.

Also on the market is the 'pram-pushchair' which is made like a pram but can be converted to a push chair by lowering the end. You can also buy buggies, cot transporters and pram-pushchairs with their own carry cots that slip into the pushchair frame which makes it very easy to cart a baby around in all sorts of situations. All pram buggies, push chairs and carry cots should have points on their inner

sides where you can fix a harness for securing the baby.

Pushchairs By the time a baby gets to six months or so you will need a pushchair or stroller. If you buy one before this age, get the variety that allows him to lie right back.

The standard type of push chair is heavy and, although it collapses down for storage or for putting in a car boot or trunk, it is difficult to manage on buses and trains. It is, however, very sturdy and will withstand a good deal of wear and tear.

The lighter, and much less expensive, version is the buggy which is easier to carry and to manoeuvre and which folds up for travelling but won't stand up quite as well to hard everyday use. Whichever type you buy, you will need a waterproof hood and apron. Always remember that your child must be strapped in with a *separate* safety harness. The T-shaped webbing or fabric (that goes round the baby's waist and between his legs) which is attached to many buggies is not strong enough for an active baby.

Do not hang shopping bags on the handles of lightweight buggies — they may tip up. Only carry shopping if the manufacturers advise that this is possible.

Baby carriers If you will be using public transport a good deal, a baby carrier is essential. Because it leaves

your hands free you'll also find it very useful for shopping and for keeping your baby close to you while you are doing various jobs. Some are available with a waterproof cover for rainy days. It is essential to buy a baby carrier/sling with a good support for the head of newborn and very young babies. There is at least one make on the market which is adjustable and can be made larger as the baby grows. Look for models with plenty of padding to go across your shoulders.

Bouncing cradles Most tiny babies can be kept contented for some time in a bouncing cradle. This is basically a fabric seat stretched across a lightweight metal frame light enough to be moved around from room to room. The baby reclines on it, held secure by a shaped strap and has a good view of what is going on around because there are no sides and because he is at an angle rather than lying flat.

Instead of, or as well as, a bouncing cradle, you can buy a highchair with a detachable seat for easy transport. Some types can be hung from the highchair frame to make a first swing. Never put any sort of detachable chair or bouncing cradle anywhere but on the floor. There have been several accidents where babies have gently bounced off tables.

FURNITURE WITH A FUTURE

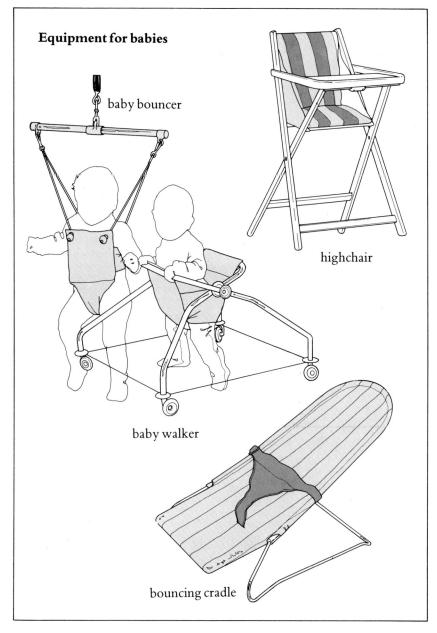

Equipment for babies

baby bouncer

highchair

baby walker

bouncing cradle

Portable highchairs and car seats Some highchairs will convert to a child's chair and table set which can be folded up for travelling (or you could always make do with the travelling pushchair or buggy). Or you can buy special baby seats that fix on to a table and can be packed flat when not in use. Other seats can be attached to an ordinary dining chair to raise the child up to adult dining height — never leave a child unattended in this sort of chair.

Up to six months a baby will travel happily and safely in a car in a carry cot fastened to the back seat with a special harness. After six months you can put him in a car safety seat with safety harness. Fabric-covered seats are more expensive but they are cosier. Always buy models which conform to the appropriate safety standards and attach them to the back seat with special fixings. It is not safe or legal to let babies ride in the front seat, even on their mothers' laps. Indeed it is not safe for any child to ride in the front seat, until he or she is big enough to use an adult seat belt.

Baby walkers There are several different types of baby walkers on the market, designed not so much to help or encourage a baby to walk but more to give him or her the chance to enjoy moving around quickly. There's a frustrating stage when they can only sit and crawl and obviously want to be more mobile and a baby walker bridges this gap very nicely.

Baby walkers support the baby in a fabric or plastic seat attached to a metal frame which moves on castors. By sitting on the seat with feet on the floor, a baby can propel herself along. Some models have a bumper all round which helps to prevent the baby from jarring his or herself when he or she bumps into hard or sharp edges and minimizes damage to furniture. Some incorporate a play tray.

Other models, made of wood or rigid plastic, are more like trolleys which can be pushed along with an upright handle, but these are really a step further along the road. If you buy this more advanced walker or an animal on wheels which can be pushed or ridden on, make sure that it is stable and will not tip over.

Swings and baby bouncers Baby swings and bouncers, like baby walkers, are not purpose-built for travelling (though they can be packed very easily and will certainly keep a child amused at the other end of the journey) but they do help the child himself towards a certain mobility. Just as some babies get quite expert at making a cradle rock by kicking their feet, your baby will probably enjoy the movement of a swing as well. Some high chairs can be transformed into an indoor swing, but you can also buy a purpose-made baby swing that winds up and swings your baby gently for up to 15 minutes. The baby must be strapped in with a separate harness. It's better not to let another child push the baby unless you are there. Never leave a baby alone in such a swing.

From the age of about three months you can put a baby in a bouncer. This is a type of fabric saddle suspended on a rod held by a length of rubber attached to a chain. A clamp fixes the chain to a door frame and you can adjust the length of the chain so that when the baby is in the saddle his or her feet just touch the floor. In this way babies can bounce gently (or not so gently depending on how strong and active they are) and securely in an open doorway. It will keep them amused and at the same time develop good muscles. The doorway must be kept clear by propping the door open. Do not leave a baby alone in the bouncer and always check all the parts of the apparatus regularly for signs of wear.

Baby bouncers are not covered by British or American Standards, so it is especially important to buy one made by a reliable manufacturer.

Highchairs needn't be traditional in design. This particular example blends in perfectly with the clean, simple lines of a modern kitchen.

The ability to adapt spaces as well as attitudes is essential when children have to be taken into account, and that applies from babyhood to well into schooldays. You can plan a child's room to perfection to contain all he or she could desire, but however beautiful or fun it is, no child is going to stay cooped up there all the time; the rest of the house belongs to him or her too. So you should be prepared for the fact that certain parts of the house will be regularly used by the children.

Kitchens and Dining Rooms

When you are working in the kitchen, (and the average housewife or working couple spends a fair time in the kitchen – even more when there's a baby to feed), you don't want toddlers under your feet and school-age children running in and out to the garden. Try to organise your space so that you have an efficient working kitchen area (preferably *not* a thoroughfare) with an area within it (or an adjacent, open plan room) where children can play, away from the dangers of ovens and pans but where they can see and be seen. You may want to wheel a pram into the kitchen and later you'll need room for a

high chair, and possibly a baby walker, so if you're lucky enough to be able to install a new kitchen, think about making room for these things – it may be worth spending a little extra to get things right at the start.

In some households, the dining room doubles as a playroom or a homework room, particularly in winter if children's rooms are cold. In any case, it is worth giving children some storage space in the dining room (or another downstairs room) so that they are encouraged to put things away.

Teenagers have very different needs: you don't need to keep an eye on them as you do with very small children; they are more independent and will probably want to get away on their own or with friends in a different room from you. They'll also have hectic timetables with after-school activites and social outings which mean they'll want to eat on their own at

As children make their presence felt throughout the house allowances have to be made for them. The resilient flooring of the modern sitting-room, left, and the adjustable platform in the bathroom, right, are good examples.

A classic example of the riotous assembly of text books, souvenirs and personal treasures that children seem to attract like magnets. Setting an area aside for work in a child's bedroom should at least prevent books and pens from spreading throughout the rest of the home. If it is possible, install a handbasin in the room as well. This enables teenagers to experiment with make-up and hair-styles without monopolizing the family bathroom and disrupting the rest of the poor long-suffering household. Here the white basin and tiles are set in a recess of a terracotta-red and cream room. The red is picked up in the paintwork which extends from above the picture rail to cover the ceiling.

different times from the rest of the family; a quiet eating area, a corner or bar arrangement in the kitchen comes in useful here.

Washing arrangements

A growing family puts a great strain on one bathroom, particularly in the mornings during the rush to work or school. It pays dividends in saved tempers if you can plumb a wash-basin into the children's room at an early age. When they are babies it will be useful for changing nappies and washing and by the time they reach school age it will shorten the queue for the bathroom. For the same reason it makes sense to provide a lavatory separate from the bathroom if you do not have one already. Alternatively, if the master bedroom is large, it might be possible to divide it so that there is a bathroom en suite for the use of parents. Even a shower cubicle in a bedroom could make life easier.

Another idea is to build in a shower, washbasin and lavatory (if there's room) under the stairs — great for removing the dirt from a child who has been playing in a sandpit or even for a shower after gardening, and it all helps to lessen the load on the upstairs bathroom.

Living room

There are two ways you can regard the living room. Either it's the warm heart of the house, cheerful, noisy, cluttered, where everybody congregates — children, parents, friends, visitors, pets, or it's a quiet retreat kept as child-free as possible most of the time and only invaded by the whole family on special occasions. If your house is a very spacious one then there are no problems keeping the living room as a refuge. If it's a small house and you do not want the children to spend all their time in the living room then it is important to make other parts of the house — their bedrooms, the dining room, a big kitchen or breakfast room — as attractive and welcoming to them as possible. Also, early on, learn to make the living room childproof to toddlers by seeing that their belongings don't dominate the scene. Provide some storage with the proviso that it's for special toys, perhaps brought in from time to time from the bedroom cupboard so that you don't have to live with perpetual clutter. A wicker basket is ideal for this purpose; it can be put out of sight quite easily. Later, a shelf or shelves in a cupboard might be better. If children use your stereo system when they are older, provide special separate storage for their records and tapes.

Extensions

If your home seems too small for all this but you don't want to move you might consider various kinds of

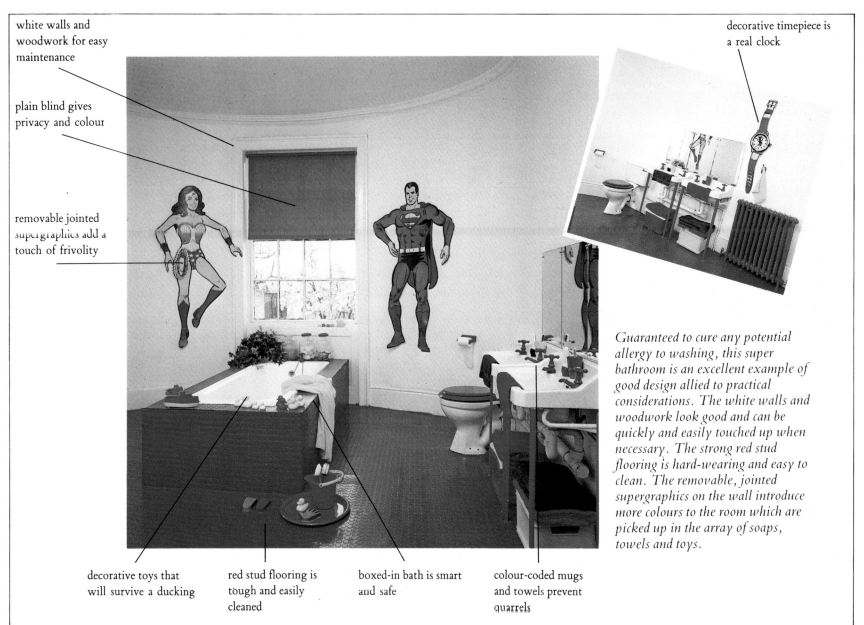

white walls and woodwork for easy maintenance

plain blind gives privacy and colour

removable jointed supergraphics add a touch of frivolity

decorative timepiece is a real clock

decorative toys that will survive a ducking

red stud flooring is tough and easily cleaned

boxed-in bath is smart and safe

colour-coded mugs and towels prevent quarrels

Guaranteed to cure any potential allergy to washing, this super bathroom is an excellent example of good design allied to practical considerations. The white walls and woodwork look good and can be quickly and easily touched up when necessary. The strong red stud flooring is hard-wearing and easy to clean. The removable, jointed supergraphics on the wall introduce more colours to the room which are picked up in the array of soaps, towels and toys.

105

extension. You can build upwards: convert a loft space into an extra bedroom or playroom. You can build outwards, adding a side extension, an extension over a garage or an extra room at the back of the house. And in some older style houses there is a basement or half basement which can be excavated further, waterproofed and turned into a serviceable playroom. Before starting on any building work consult a professional. You may have to get planning permission or satisfy the Borough Surveyor that your plans and building are sound.

If you are building an extra room in any of these ways you can ensure from the word go that they are really soundproof and well insulated against heat loss too. You will also need to make sure that there is adequate ventilation.

Adapting the furnishings

While there are children around it is not a good idea to indulge in pale or delicate upholstery and soft furnishings unless they are easily wash-

An alternative to moving for the expanding family is to find 'room at the top'. Here a converted loft provides plenty of room for sleep and play areas, which are clearly defined by changes in flooring and wall covering. The entire room has been cleverly colour-coordinated in this pleasing and practical space.

able. This doesn't mean you are condemned to have all covers, curtains and carpets in sturdy, serviceable weights and dark, dirt-proof colours but rather that you choose finishes as much for their wearability and cleanability as their aesthetic effect.

Floors in kitchens and dining rooms should be easy to wipe clean. It is not a good idea to have carpet in a dining room where young children are going to be eating regularly. Newspaper or a sheet of plastic under the chair help. Walls, too, are going to take a lot of punishment and will need to withstand repeated cleaning. If you do have nonwashable or non-wipeable wallpaper, have it coated with clear polyurethane so that you can sponge it down when necessary.

On the whole, blinds are always better and safer than trailing curtains because there is nothing a small child can trip over or pull down so long as cords are kept well out of reach.

If you have any reasonably big ground floor room in a house or apartment (it is not advisable to consider it on an upper floor in any building), it's worth covering the floor in tough, easy-care vinyl, linoleum, cork or composition tiles of one kind or another. A good tough floor will not show marks, or at least will not retain them, and you will find it a boon on rainy days for

tricyling and even roller skating.

Remember that stairs provide an endless source of fascination and play for children once they get a little older. They will almost inevitably want to slide down banisters, push themselves on their tummies down the stairs or try to walk up the outside of the steps beyond the banisters. You can't do much to prevent this but you can make sure that the stairs and the floor below are well carpeted and hand rails are smooth and splinter free.

Adapting a room

Adapting one room to take a second child is different again. It helps if you start off designing the room with the possibility of more children in mind rather than try to squash later children into a room obviously planned for one. The main thing is to give each child a certain amount of privacy without sacrificing too much of the general play space and there are lots of ways of doing this, depending on the size and shape of the space you have.

Above right: An attractive loft conversion which has well-lit work surfaces and good storage under the raised bed and below the eaves.

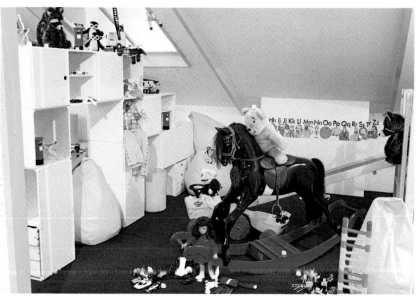

Right: The white room divider in this well-planned attic makes use of all the available space as well as providing versatile storage.

Room at the top

Good use has been made here of the loft, a large and often wasted area that makes an ideal den. Planning permission and the advice of an architect are usually needed to convert an attic, but it is often well worth a little trouble and expense for the extra living space. Once the building work was completed, very little outlay was needed to create a multi-purpose room. The roof was insulated and covered in polyurethaned tongue-and-groove boards, with sloping louvred windows screened by bright red blinds. The plain white plasterboard walls, with one wall left bare brick and painted white for a change of texture, add to the light effect. Black storage units raised on a platform at the far end and bright red platform sofas along two walls create a touch of drama, the sofas doubling as beds with large foam cushions in a striking red, black and grey fabric and storage drawers below. The sturdy floor is well insulated and covered in hard-wearing coir matting to take the punishment of punch-ball, exercise bike, drum kit and synthesizer, and there is still plenty of room for hi-fi equipment, small tv and computer console. With a kettle for tea and coffee, large floor cushions in matching fabrics and a ceiling fan to cool the air in summer, this loft is the perfect retreat for teenagers.

Adapting for sharing

There are some situations in which you may need to make a physical barrier in a room where children are sharing, – for instance when two teenagers or school-age children of the opposite sex share. Curtains or an old fashioned Victorian screen, re-vamped as a double sided pin board may be enough to divide sleeping areas. Or you can make a more solid barrier with furniture – two wardrobes, backed with posters, put end to end between the sleeping areas, with a door facing each bed, makes a removable room divider. You can make a lower barrier by putting the desks, made up from work tops placed over chests, as described in the first chapter, between the beds. By fixing a board to the back of each desk you can create more solid dividers, and provide private workspace at the same time. If space is more limited, build double-sided or open bookshelves between the beds as a divider.

If you can't provide physically separated areas, at least define the space, so that each child has his or her own storage area, display area, playspace and so on. For instance, in a room with alcoves on either side of a chimney breast, try to allocate

Left: A purpose-designed room divider which gives each child an equal area for sleep, play and storage in a minimal space.

one alcove to each child. You can build in a desk top with storage below and a noticeboard and shelves above. Choose one colour for each child, and follow the theme through with painted shelves, bedlinen, towels, toy boxes and so on.

Although parents usually take the largest bedroom as theirs, it often makes better sense to use the second bedroom as the main bedroom and give the largest room to the children, so that they have more space for their activities and can spend more time there. It also gives you more scope for dividing the room and giving them some privacy.

Adapting the room, or rooms, as they grow older and develop their own tastes is different again. If you have followed the staged plan suggested at the beginning of the book, the gradual changes won't be nearly as traumatic as a sudden transformation into a whole new room. The basic bones, the main bulk of the furniture, will be there, leaving plenty of space and scope for the teenager to stamp it with his or her own personality.

Even if you hate what your teenagers do to that former pretty or cute little room, try to ignore it; it's more important that each individual learns to express their tastes and they will only grow and improve in this respect by being able to experiment in the first place. If you really can't stand it, just shut the door

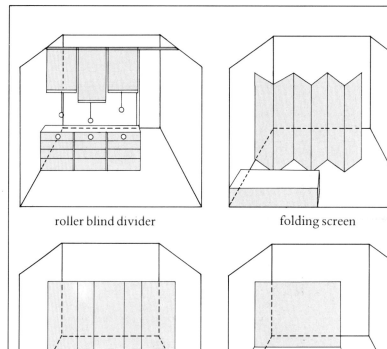

roller blind divider

folding screen

Japanese mobile screen

internal partition wall

Room dividers

All children need a space they can call their own. If you are unable to give each child a room of his or her own, then it's a good idea to provide some sort of barrier which will define territory and afford each child a degree of privacy. Dividers can also be used to split off a work/play area from a sleeping area. Top left: A long chest of drawers is a permanent fixture, while roller blinds can be pulled down to form a screen as required. Top right: A folding screen can be used for posters too. Bottom left: Sliding Japanese rice paper screens cut out less light. Bottom right: An internal partition wall is permanent but gives greater privacy.

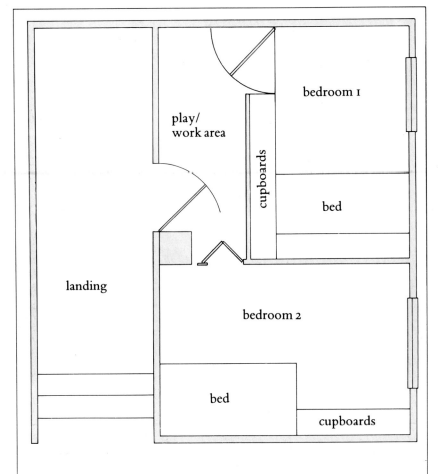

bedroom 1

play/
work area

cupboards

bed

landing

bedroom 2

bed

cupboards

Two into one will go

If you have a sufficiently large bedroom, then one solution to the problems arising from brothers and sisters sharing a room is to divide it up. Here, internal partition walls have been erected in an L-shape so that each child has a small bedroom *with one window, cupboards and the privacy afforded by an individual door. A communal play/work area has also been created which can be used for homework, book-shelves, tv, desk, computer and so on.*

firmly and don't go in. Sooner or later it will probably get into such a muddle that even the teenager will want to do something about it. It shouldn't be a constant battle ground. They and you will learn that the hard way but it is worth it in the long run; if you respect their possessions and space they are far more likely to come to respect them too.

Finding the space for one more

No-one needs to be told that in a small house or flat or apartment it is not going to be easy to find space for one more child. But here are some suggestions:

● Make a partition wall three-quarters of the way down the child's bedroom. Furnish one side with two bunkbeds and a desk to give just the right amount of privacy for the older child (or children); the rest can be play and sleeping space for the new arrival. Line the wall with blackboard or pin or bulletin board, or with shelves.

● Build a hardboard room within a room with the outside walls all shelves and a cantilevered panel which lets down to become a table or pushes up to become a bulletin board.

● For another room-within-a-room, build a work/storage sleeping unit with white-laminate plastic surfaces, or in painted wood. This frees the perimeter of the room to make it look more spacious.

● Build in a wall of storage and work surfaces including a Murphy bed for an older child. This will fold up during the daytime to make more play space.

Safety precautions

It is important to think about safety, especially in areas like the kitchen and living room where children will spend a lot of time with you.

Hall, stairs and corridors

● Make sure that lighting in corridors and on stairs and steps is adequate at all times of day and night.

● Use a non-slip polish if your hall floor is wood or tiled.

● See that stair carpets are well fitting with no loose or worn parts to catch on or trip over.

● Fix a gate to the top and bottom of the stairs *before* your child starts to crawl and explore. Make sure that safety barriers placed in doorways or at the top and bottom of staircases comply with the requirements of BS 4125.

Right: This bedroom is designed for two children to have space at either end for clothes storage, seating, sleeping – and even a bed for a friend to sleep toe-to-toe overnight. Happily, there is still room in the middle for play.

Kitchens
- Make sure that kettle spouts and saucepan handles are turned inwards on to the stove.
- Keep doors on freezers, refrigerators, washing machines and tumble dryers firmly closed and discourage any climbing on such machinery.
- Don't leave any appliances, particularly chip pans and deep fat pans, unattended.
- Wipe up spills on floors at once.
- Ensure cleaning materials and all dangerous household substances are kept well out of reach of children. Fit childproof locks to under-work surface cupboards if necessary. At the moment there are no regulations for child-resistant containers for dangerous household substances, but they are expected very shortly.
- Ensure that there are no flexes trailing round the kitchen: sockets should be positioned behind the work surface if at all possible.

Living rooms
- Guard the windows. If you have unbarred windows make sure the bottom part is never open when there are children around. Provide all windows with childproof locks.
- Put fireguards around fires and fireplaces and *never* leave a child alone in a room with a fire.
- Use childproof sockets for electrical fittings and do not have any trailing flexes or wires that could cause accidents.
- Move any arrangements of small objects on low tables to a higher level for the time being.
- Glass doors should be fitted with safety glass or safety film so that if it is banged it will not splinter. Glaziers who are members of the Glass and Glazing Federation will advise on appropriate glazing for particular sizes and locations.

Bathrooms
- See that all fittings and switches comply with the relevant special safety regulations.
- Never leave children alone in a bath or in the bathroom.
- Lock up medicines and pills at all times in a cabinet well out of reach.
- Never keep any portable electric appliances in the bathroom.
- Provide an adjustable platform or footstool to enable children to reach the sink and lavatory.
- Remove all door locks at child-height to avoid children locking themselves in.
- Put lavatory cleaners, bleaches and detergents in a cupboard with a childproof lock.

General
- Make sure that cupboards and closets which could be tipped or pulled over are fixed to the wall. Any other potentially dangerous free-standing furniture should be moved out of harm's way.
- Keep flooring firmly fixed down, particularly in doorways.
- Tidy away toys on the floor to prevent people tripping up.

Safety features

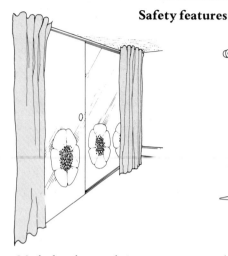

Mark glass doors and picture windows with a bright, noticeable sticker

A moveable steel safety gate suitable for doors and stairways

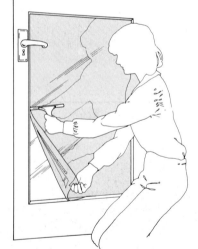

Fit doors and windows with safety film to prevent splintering glass

An adjustable wooden safety gate permanently fixed to the staircase

More than half the accidents that occur in the home involve children under the age of five. A relatively small outlay on some essential pieces of safety equipment could help you avoid such accidents.

Left, top: A strong wall-mounted fireguard is essential for rooms with wall-mounted gas and electric fires. Most models have sides which open for easy access to controls.

Left, above: For open fireplaces you need an extending fireguard with an adjustable width. These too fold flat for storage. Fireguards are also available for cabinet heaters which are fitted with castors. Neither fireguards nor heater guards should be used to air clothes or bedding.

Centre, top: Buy a hob guard with telescopic front and side panels to give a secure fit on most hob-type cookers. Always ensure that pan handles are pointed inwards to avoid scalding.

Centre, above: A battery-operated baby alarm, with volume control, provides two-way communication between you and your baby. If baby is crying in another room you can comfort him or her by speaking.

Right, top: Electric shock can kill or burn. To prevent a child poking objects or fingers into electric points, switch off and cover unused points with a safety cover. Put away all electrical appliances after use.

Right, above: A childproof lock will prevent nimble little fingers from opening a window. Keep the key nearby, in case of fire.

THE GARDEN IS A ROOM TOO

Since children grow like trees there is little point in designing a whole garden especially for them. Nevertheless, there are all sorts of ways of adapting a garden or yard, whatever its dimensions so that it becomes both safer and more attractive for children to play in. Such a garden must cater for the often conflicting needs of adults, children and sometimes pets too, whether rabbits in hutches or an energetic dog. In addition to a lawn and plant beds, there should ideally be space for bicycle storage, hanging out the washing and possibly growing some fruit, vegetables and herbs as well.

Essentially gardens are places of enjoyment, both in terms of peace and relaxation for parents and the freedom for their children to be noisy and boisterous. A well thought out garden can satisfy all those demands.

If you have the room for a patio or paved area, this will provide a place to sit when the grass is damp as well as a practical area for outdoor eating. Site a sandpit here, where it is visible from a kitchen window say, and you will be able to sweep back the sand easily afterwards, if necessary, and keep an eye on young children while cooking.

If there *is* space in, say, a country garden to make a sort of adventure playground, it's well worth sacrificing some of the acreage or leaving some of the wilder bits to them. And if the children can create much of the environment themselves, that's better still. They will soon see the possibilities for discovering secret passages and hideaways in the bushes, digging tunnels, making a tree house and so on. Under guidance, they can plant trees, shrubs and other plants, grow cuttings and vegetables themselves.

Adventure playgrounds

In our own garden in the country we made a rope ladder and stretched some tough rope between several tall trees. With the addition of a pulley and more rope for a swing seat my three children made a marvellous Tarzan-like swing-way which seemed to give them a thrill a foot and endless hours of amusement. But it also inspired all sorts of elaborations and with more rope,

Whatever size of garden you may have, it can make a useful extra room for children to play in, left, or eat in, right, without the restrictions they face indoors.

THE GARDEN IS A ROOM TOO

sacks, old logs and branches, a trampoline, an original climbing frame, and goodness knows what else, they constructed a complicated edifice which was jungle-walkway, endurance test and tree-house all in one, culminating in an area for a camp fire and a tent where they could cook their own sausages and sleep out if they wanted to. This, of course, proves the theory that the desire to build is instinctive in most children and is a basis for many forms of early learning. The experience of building gives them the opportunity to make a world equal in their minds to their parents' world, and better still, to make a place of their own that they feel comfortable in.

Adventure versus safety

Of course, the whole concept of adventure playgrounds, of giving children the opportunity to test themselves and their endurance, their building skills and their imagination, is not necessarily compatible with the safety stressed throughout this book. All the same, there is a happy medium, somewhere between courting danger and finding things out for oneself; between being careful and cautious about hazards and developing confidence and self-reliance. And even if the garden is a city garden, without benefit of trees and bushes and undergrowth, amazing things can

be constructed from conventional climbing frames and swings, tarpaulins and ground sheets and sand pits, with, of course, the same regard for safety.

Children's space versus adults' pleasure

However splendid it is to be able to give children their head and the opportunities to create their own play environment, the fact remains that few of us have the space to give over much of the garden entirely to children. If there is a garden at all, adults will want to use it too. Moreover their expectations of it will be not only different but often in direct opposition to those of their children: they will want it to be a pleasant place for sitting out or just looking at or for indulging their creative talents as gardeners. So the garden and its equipment need to be as adaptable as possible to suit both camps — a tall order. It requires a certain amount of forethought and careful planning if it has to be attractive, safe and a good place for playing. You may have to make some temporary compromises and shelve some garden 'dreams' for the time being but a family garden can be made to work to everybody's advantage without putting a damper on children's self expression.

It means planning with one eye on the future so that when the swings and tree house days are over,

Left: Even if you are not lucky enough to have a garden you can make excellent use of a balcony. This area incorporates storage for toys, seating, a sandpit with cover, rails and a net to act as a safety precaution and prevent the disappearance of playthings over the side, tough canvas blinds to keep out the elements and even a blackboard.

Above: The frame of this well-constructed wooden swing forms part of a pergola and when the swing is removed in later years, it will support climbing plants.

Right: A wooden-framed sandpit is an inexpensive play/sitting area.

the garden can go back to being a proper garden again with the minimum of rearrangement or structural upheaval.

Good forward thinking

● A sandpit could be installed in a part of the garden where it can be turned into a pond or small bed later. It needn't be an eyesore, as you will need to cover it to protect it from rain, leaves, cats, etc. Arrange it so that the cover serves some useful purpose and is not ugly to look at. You could, for example, have some cotton or canvas-covered blocks of foam rubber made so that it can be turned into an agreeable seating area when the children have gone to bed (or grown older) and the weather is good enough for sitting outside. Use sharp sand and not builder's sand, which dries out more quickly and does not clog or stain.

● Swings are fun but can take their toll of a lawn and dominate the landscape. If possible, site them, firmly anchored, where they will not entirely ruin the ground underneath or the view. Do not put them on a bit of lawn that is in full view unless you have planted it with specially tough grass. You can put them over a path as long as you

Left: Conventional climbing frames and swings can be constructed, with due regard for safety, to help children develop confidence and self-reliance.

provide a large mat underneath to cushion falls. And left-over swings with the actual chain or rope and seat removed, can provide the basis for climbing plants such as vines, honeysuckle or roses later on.

• A wall or a strong fence can be put to good use for tennis practice: draw a line along it at tennis net height. Later you can plant quick-growing climbers like polygonum or jasmine to cover it.

• The hedge should not become a burial ground for lost balls. Consider buying the sort of tough hedging plants that will bounce balls back, rather than letting them go straight through. Ask your local nursery garden or supplier for advice on this.

• Forget about velvet lawns for a few years. Go for the special child-proof or cricket-type mix of lawn seed which is much tougher than the ordinary variety. If you can afford it, make a hard surface for children to cycle on.

• Try to give the children their own bit of garden. Even if the whole area is quite small, you can still spare a bit for them. Fence off an end with trellis covered in thick polygonum or Russian vine which grows thick and fast, or honey-suckle or other thornless climber, and you will nicely hide the Wendy houses, wigwams, sandpits, adventure structures and so on from immediate view.

Growing interests

It is quite possible to reconcile your demands from a garden with those of your children. A sand pit, (above right) can later be used as an additional bedding area. As children develop, you could provide them with a garden house of their own and encourage a mutual respect of territories. This need not be expensive. The one shown on the right was made of old fruit boxes and camembert packets . . . If you can encourage your children to take a more active interest, as above, by giving them a plot of their own, you should both reap rewards.

Left and above: If you are unable to extend your home upwards or outwards, it might be worthwhile considering the garage. Natural light has been introduced here by glazing the doors, and is supplemented by fluorescent tubes. Quarry tiles provide a floor which is easy to clean and strong enough to withstand a car. The walls have been painted white and covered with prints and posters to make them lighter and brighter. All storage for books and toys has been neatly positioned to one side to allow access for the car, and plenty of space for children to play in when the garage is not in use.

Right: A quarry-tiled conservatory, with a radiator for chilly days, is a terrific play space for children when it's too wet to play outside. Note also the durable cycle track in the garden.

• Summer houses make marvellous play-spaces for children as well as providing accessible storage space for bikes and toys, and later come into their own as sheltered sitting-out places. Locate them so that there is hidden-away space at the back for a children-only area.

• Fruit trees can act as climbing frames as well as contributing useful produce in years to come.

Garages and sheds

Garages and sheds make terrific extra play spaces for children too. So long as they are carefully arranged and planned with any potentially harmful tools, chemicals or liquids locked away or put right out of reach. Parallel bars, for example, can be fixed to walls for gym practice. A collapsible table tennis or billiard table can be brought out when the car is gone. A long table can be fixed up at one end for model-making. Ropes for swinging on can be attached to the overhead beams, as can trapezes, and ropes with tyres attached (but do not leave young children unattended where there are hanging ropes about).

Even a small garden shed can be partitioned inside to provide space for the storage of garden tools, bicycles and so forth, on one side, while the other half can act as a small playroom – ideal for rainy days. Train children not to bring their outside things into the house.

The safety aspects

You can only turn children loose in the garden with any peace of mind if you make it safe for them. These are the potential hazards:

• *Water* — in ponds, streams, lily ponds, swimming pools. See that they are covered, if possible, or fenced off. Teach children to swim at the earliest possible moment.

Remember that even a few centimetres (inches) of water is enough for a child to drown in.

• If you have greenhouses and glass cloches keep children away from them or consider plastic as an alternative. Fence or hedge them off and make them a no-go area.

• Keep washing lines out of easy reach. If possible use one of those umbrella-like rotary lines instead, which can be put safely away when not in use.

• Avoid all poisonous plants with leaves or berries children might pick and eat. The following plants are poisonous to children and pets if eaten in moderate amounts. Plants marked with an asterisk are extremely poisonous: aconite★, box, columbine, daphne★, foxglove★, hellebore★, honeysuckle berries, ivy, laburnum★, oleander★, privet, spindle-tree, spurge, yew★.

In addition, all members of the *Ranunculus* family are poisonous.

• Screen off part of the garden for pets to use as excreta can carry dangerous germs.

123

Accent colours Contrast colours used to spice up room schemes and to draw attention to chosen objects.

Acetate A thin sheet of transparent, plastic-like material. A design can be cut out of the sheet for making a stencil.

Airbrick A perforated brick set into a wall to allow ventilation.

Baby bouncer A saddle suspended from a rod which is attached to a length of rubber and adjustable chain. This is clamped to a door frame and the door propped open. The chain is adjusted so that a baby in the saddle is able to touch the floor with his feet. The bouncer is useful both for keeping a baby amused and exercising his muscles.

Baby walker A metal frame on castors in which a baby can propel himself, supported by a seat.

Baffle A narrow screen or partition placed so as to hinder or control the passage of light or sound.

Batten A strip of wood. Fixed to the wall at intervals, a series of battens can be used to attach panelling, insulation board or fabric.

Bouncing cradle A reclining seat into which a baby can be securely held by a strap. The fabric seat is fixed to a lightweight metal frame, which is placed on the floor.

BSI British Standards Institution. An independent body which sets standards for the safety and performance of many consumer products. These may be invoked by government regulations but manufacturers generally use them voluntarily. For further information contact Public Relations Department, British Standards Institution, 2 Park Street, London W1A 2BS.

Café curtain A short curtain hung from a rod going half way across a window, as in French cafés. It is sometimes hung in a double tier, and is a useful treatment for windows that open inwards or face the street.

Cantilever A projection from the wall.

Chair or dado rail Wooden moulding, lengths of which can be attached to the wall to make a dado.

Chipboard Board made from compressed softwood chips and resin.

Dado The lower part of a wall separated by a rail known as the dado or chair rail.

Dimmer switch A knob (or rheostat) or panel that is used to control brightness of light. It saves energy as well as giving a flexible range of lighting levels.

Frieze A decorative, horizontal band or border along a wall or dado. The frieze could be painted, stencilled or composed of cut-outs.

High tech Contemporary style using industrial components adapted for domestic use.

Laminate A very strong multi-layered material.

Moses basket The simplest and oldest form of carry cot, an oblong-shaped basket with handles. Also useful as a container for storage.

Mural A decorative scene, realistic or fantastic, painted directly on to a wall.

Murphy bed A bed that lets down from the wall against which it is concealed when not in use.

Nursing chair Low, comfortable chair usually without arms. The ideal form of seating for nursing and feeding a baby.

Pelmet or valance A decorative, horizontal band of fabric usually attached to the top of a window frame to hide rods and provide added interest.

Pendant lighting Light which hang from the ceiling.

Pinboard A board, usually made of cork, on which papers or pictures can be attached with pins.

Pinoleum or matchstick blind A blind made from very thin wooden reeds.

Quarry tiles Fired tiles made from unrefined clays which provide very durable flooring. They are impervious to grease and liquids, and come in a range of muted colours.

Roller blind A fabric blind which is controlled by a spring mechanism.

Roman blind One that draws up into neat horizontal folds by means of cords threaded through rings attached at regular intervals to the back of the fabric. You can either use rings alone, or on heavier fabrics, you can attach light battens to keep the folds crisp. Ideal for a smooth, tailored effect.

Scrap-screen Popular in the Victorian era, this was made of hinged panels onto which scraps and cut-outs were pasted, then varnished over.

Skirting or base board Wooden board attached to the base of a wall as a protection against kicking and scuffing.

Spotlight A light that directs a strong, controlled beam of light on to an object or place. Can be fixed or adjustable.

Stencil A decorative design which is cut out of acetate or waxed paper, then reproduced onto a surface beneath it with paint using a brush or spray can.

Tarpaulin Waterproofed canvas sheeting, used for protecting or covering large objects or surfaces.

Task lighting Light for reading, or work or play surfaces. Lights should be angled directly onto the book or whatever work is in progress.

Tog A measurement of heat insulation. Tog ratings are used to indicate the warmth of continental quilts or duvets. The higher the tog, the warmer the duvet will be.

Tongue-and-groove panelling Wood panelling, where the boards are interlocked along the edges.

Track lighting A length of track along which a number of light fittings can be positioned and supplied by one electrical outlet. It can be mounted on any wall or ceiling surface, or recessed.

Trompe l'oeil Anything which deceives the eye.

Truckle bed A low bed on castors or wheels for rolling under another bed.

Valance see Pelmet. Also the decorative length of fabric which covers the sides of a bed.

Velcro A patented fastener consisting of two fabric strips, one with a velvety surface, the other with tiny hooks. When pressed together the two strips cling.

Venetian blind A pull-up blind made with horizontal slats that can be adjusted to let in or exclude light.

Yacht paint A tough, hard-wearing paint, also known as deck paint, used on boats or to paint wood floors.

ACKNOWLEDGMENTS

The author and publishers would particularly like to thank the following people and companies for their contribution to this book:

for their invaluable help and research work: Deborah Evans, Yvonne Rees and Rachel Duffield

for technical advice: The British Standards Institution

for allowing us to photograph their homes: Daphne Boyce, Shellard Campbell, Sisi Edmiston, Jane Gibbard, Diana Kelion, Carol Magowan, Charles and Annabel Merullo, Jenny Raworth, Carol Thomas, Ruth Thomson, Susie Usiskin.

for supplying merchandise for the room sets: Afia Carpets, Mary Fox Linton, Marks and Spencer plc and Paper Moon.

for supplying props for special photography: Athena Posters, Clifton Nurseries, Descamps, Designers Guild, Hippo Hall, Lunn Antiques, Maison Designs Ltd, Marks and Spencer plc, The General Store Covent Garden, The Kite Store, The Reject Shop, Tiger-Tiger.

Black and white line illustrations by Stuart Perry. Colour illustrations by Ross Wardle/Tudor Art Studios and Ken Hollins.

Special photography
Michael Dunne: (designer Diana Kelion) 24 above right, 36 left, 37, 38, 49, 52, 55 below, 58, 60, 61, 62, 64 above right, (architect Pamela Banchero Associates and builder John Potter Interiors) 76, 91 below right, 94 above left and right, 95, 104, 105, (designer Diana Kelion) 106.

Jon Bouchier: back jacket

David Johnson: 22/23, 66/67, 74/75, 108/109

The publishers wish to thank the following organisations and individuals for their kind permission to reproduce the photographs in this book: Alno Kitchens 101; Jon Bouchier/EWA (architect Michael Tilley) 113; Michael Boys/Susan Griggs Agency Ltd 12 below right, 19, 47 above right, 71, 73 above left, (designer John Stefanidis) 73 below right, 103, 110; Richard Bryant/Arcaid 14, 15 right; Karl Bühler/EWA 120; Karl-Dietrich Bühler (designer Dick Huigens) 116, 119 left; Camera Press 12 above left and right, below left, 13, 20, 21, 24, 34, 39 above, 59, 68, 69, 77, 79, 80 left, 81, 88, 89, 92, 97 right, 99, 107 above, 118; Chubb Security Services Ld 115 below right; Cover Plus Paints/F.W. Woolworth 54; David Cripps/EWA 47 below left; Design Council 107 below; Dorma 17, 35 below, 40, 53 left, 91 above; Dragons of Walton Street 36 right; Dreamline Fitted Bedrooms 72; Michael Dunne-EWA 43, 98; Richard Einzig/Arcaid 41; Faber Blinds 65; Geofrey Frosh/EWA 47 right; Clive Helm/EWA 55 above, (designer Gabbi Tubbs) 123; Hippo Hall 35 above left; ICI Paints 28; Interior Selection 56; International Wool Secretariat 57; Ken Kirkwood 24 below right, 25 above right; David Lloyd/EWA 83; Maison Designs Ltd 91 below left; Maison de Marie Claire/Dirand/Olry 18, 124; Maison de Marie Claire/Eriaud/Comte 6, 82; Maison de Marie Claire/Ptaut/Puech 2, 4–5, 16, 26; Marks and Spencer plc 15 left, 90; Norman McGrath 29, 30, (designer Noel Jeffrey) 31, 33 above left, (designer Noel Jeffrey) 33 below right, (designer Michelle Clifton) 35 above right, (designer Caroline Levy) 42; Meredew Furniture Ltd 70; Mothercare 115 above left, centre right, below centre and left; Michael Nicholson/EWA 9; Julian Nieman/EWA (designer Sara Starkey) 55 above left, (architect Peter Bell and Partners) 122; Spike Powell/EWA (designers Vivien and Hamish Pringle) 32, 63; Malcolm Robertson/Home Improvement Guides 102; Stag Cabinet Company 8; Jessica Strang (designer Jessica Strang) 73 above right, (designer Chris Penfold) 78 below; Tim Street-Porter/EWA 45 above and below right; Transworld Feature Syndicate (Elyse Lewin) 39 below, 50, 51, 53 right, 64 left, 78 above left and right, 80 right, 85, 94 below, 96, 97 left, 121 above and below left; Jerry Tubby/EWA 121 above right; Elizabeth Whiting and Associates 45 below left, 93, 117, 119 right.

INDEX